PEOPLE NOT PAPERCLIPS

PUTTING THE HUMAN
BACK INTO HUMAN RESOURCES

Kath Howard

First published in Great Britain by Practical Inspiration Publishing, 2020

The moral rights of the author have been asserted

ISBN   978-1-78860-133-7 (print)
         978-1-78860-132-0 (epub)
         978-1-78860-131-3 (mobi)

Every effort has been made to trace copyright holders and to obtain their permission for the use of copyright material. The publisher apologizes for any errors or omissions and would be grateful if notified of any corrections that should be incorporated in future reprints or editions of this book.

Practical Inspiration
PUBLISHING

Contents

Foreword

There is a reason why we don't pay particular attention to paperclips – we view them as a commodity, and we treat them as such. With an endless supply of paperclips available on the market, we don't care where they came from and what's unique about them – as long as they do their job well. When one gets bent out of shape and is no longer useful, we swiftly replace it with another one – no drama, no tears, no second thoughts.

Now, try replacing the word 'paperclips' in the paragraph above with the word 'people'. Shocking? Certainly. But, sadly, not that far from the stark reality many employees experience today. In our attempt to drive business results and shareholder value, we seem to have forgotten that our workforce consists of living, breathing human beings. No wonder that only one in ten Brits feels engaged at work and more than two million think of quitting their job every single day. The way we think about work is broken and it's time we take action and stop treating people as if they were paperclips.

Kath Howard's book, *People Not Paperclips: Putting the Human Back into Human Resources*, comes at a time when we desperately need some guidance on how to fix our broken HR systems and bring humanity to the workplace. It brings invaluable insights from the field of Organisational Design, Organisational Psychology, and over 20 years of Kath's practical experience in the world of business and HR. The question at the centre of Kath's book is: 'How can we build healthy, people-centred cultures that drive results and allow people to flourish?'

This book is not for everyone. It's not for those who are on the lookout for yet another exciting fad, a quick fix, or an idea for a short-term intervention that will cause some stir and fizzle out before it's over. It's not for the well-meaning enthusiast who lacks the patience to grapple with the reality of our businesses and our humanity.

It's a book for people who seek sustainable change and who need a better understanding of how to integrate organisational design, behavioural science, evidence-based practice and systems thinking into their HR practice. It's an invaluable resource for those willing to test their ideas in the workplace and eager to embrace innovation as a core skill in HR.

As a culture strategist, I'm lucky to work with companies committed to creating people-centric cultures. They invest in their people because they know that it's the only way to bring their vision and business aspirations to life. Working with these organisations has taught me that change is hard. Every time you challenge the status quo, you are met by forces and dynamics that are both complex and profoundly messy.

If you want to join us on a mission to re-humanise the workplace, you'll meet these forces, too. And you will need a healthy dose of courage, inspiration and the right tools to tackle the challenge. This book is a collection of topics, references and suggestions for how you can create an HR function and an organisation that drives the change people are seeking. If you want to cultivate a 'people not paperclips' culture, dive into it, learn from it and embark on a never-ending experiment: test, learn, refine, repeat.

September 2019, Aga Bajer

Preface

I have spent over 20 years working within organisations to understand people and how they interact, and to apply this understanding to support more productive, and ultimately more fulfilling, workplaces. I describe myself on business and professional networks as a Change Agent, HR Leader, Occupational Psychologist, Facilitator, Coach and Organisation Development Consultant. I'm all of these things, but above all else, I'm a human who is interested in other humans. I derive my personal meaning from seeking to create meaning at work for others. I've worked in a wide range of industries and organisations and I've worn multiple hats as a researcher, HR practitioner, Chartered Psychologist and Consultant. Through this experience, I've observed that work just isn't working for many of us. People are often treated as a resource akin to a box of paperclips; shifting them around, using terms such as 'capital' or 'headcount', and 'managing them out' when they're no longer deemed to be productive. This book is my response to this work context. I believe there is a huge opportunity to work together to bring greater humanity into the workplace, and that both organisations and people will benefit.

I founded HeartSparks, an Organisation Development (OD) consultancy, with the purpose of sparking change in how we treat people at work. Quick fixes in recognition schemes or reward structures just aren't going to cut it any longer. We need to support holistic, sustainable change in our workplace; change that offers the opportunity to create cultures that treat people as individuals with individual needs, motivations and desires. I'm proposing that we can learn so much from the world of behavioural science and from Organisation Development when considering such a lofty aim to bring greater humanity into the workplace. We carry sizeable influence within HR, and a good starting point for creating a person-centred shift in our organisations would be to create this same shift in how we operate as a function. This book is a first step for all HR professionals to start building HR teams that will put the human back into Human Resources. As Gandhi (sort of) said, let's 'be the change we want to see in the world'.

Why am I the right person to write this book? In all honesty, as I write this, I'm knee-deep in imposter syndrome and thinking perhaps I'm not the right person at all. But no one else has written it, and I think it needs to be read. Or rather, it needs to be read, and the concepts within need to explored and talked about and acted on through every organisation that employs people. Rest assured that I have the technical expertise to speak sensibly on this topic, from leading employee engagement, talent development, OD and change leadership within major brands and government departments and spending 20 years studying or learning more as an Occupational Psychologist. And rest assured my sense of humility made me feel slightly nauseous as I just wrote that sentence. But more importantly, this topic is central to who I am, to my values and to how I operate. We'll explore the concept of 'self as an instrument' in OD within the book, but this is me using myself as an instrument or tool to guide our collective practice as HR professionals. I don't think you can truly lead and create cultural change if you don't seek to embody your vision through all you say and do. I seek to be compassionate and to bring 'heart' to my OD and HR practice, which I think puts me in a strong position to be at the very least your 'guide' in creating person-centred cultures, if not perhaps your 'guru'.

You can find out more about me and my work here: www.heartsparks.co.uk

Acknowledgements

I would like to thank so many of the amazing people I've worked with who have inspired me to write this book. From the Director of Organisation Development & People at Save the Children, Leonie Lonton, who perhaps never knew what an inspiration she was to me as my line manager during my time there. Leonie inspired me so greatly in her sheer drive to improve the lives of children, and in her ability to do so whilst always being such a genuinely kind person. And to the wonderful Pat Johnson, certainly one of the very finest colleagues and OD professionals I have worked with. Pat, you taught me so much about OD; from applying it in practice, to continuously working to develop 'myself as an instrument'. My career aspiration continues to be to work with you again, and I feel so lucky to call you a dear friend.

I also want to thank my lovely friends and family who have supported me this year, personally and professionally. I'm blessed to have known many of my friends for nearly 30 years, and they have spurred me on to write the book that follows.

I would also like to thank all the amazing people at Practical Inspiration Publishing for supporting and, at times, cajoling me toward this finished book. And most of all, to Alison Jones of Practical Inspiration Publishing. You made me realise that writing a book could be more than a dream.

This book is dedicated to all the hidden voices in organisations; the people who are quietened, aren't given the support to reach their potential or aren't treated with the dignity and compassion they deserve. There really is another way.

And finally, this book is also dedicated to my little people, Martha and Sebastian. There are times that I haven't been with you so that I could write this book. It is my small contribution to a world of work where one day I hope you'll both be valued for being the uniquely, crazily special people that you are. I hope that one day you will find work that makes your heart and head sing too.

And so the book will open with a quote from Martha's favourite story, for some of the best leadership and business lessons are to be found in stories:

Have courage and be kind.

[Cinderella, from the film, 2015]

Introduction
Who took the human out of Human Resources?

When did HR professionals decide that the key route to credibility was to be 'business-focused' and to follow a mantra where profits are placed above people? Why have so many leaders and HR professionals alike spent so long on business cases, ignoring the need for a 'person case'? The reality is that so few people-focused issues or opportunities can be reduced to a set of tangible 'results' outlined on a spreadsheet. Regardless of whether there is a strong scientific or financial argument for doing something, we might still take a course of action from the moral standpoint that it is the right thing to do.

We are living longer than ever in the Western world and will be working for more years than past generations as a result. The world of work and the jobs available to people have both changed wildly with the advent of the internet, and we're fast adapting to new ways of working in HR. Research from psychologists such as Barry Schwartz[1] suggests that people are seeking meaning from their work and careers, and that experiencing this meaning is one of the most important factors for job satisfaction. How people create meaning will depend, amongst other factors, on their motivations and personal context, but having a level of autonomy and an opportunity to develop and grow will support them in achieving meaning through their work. The informal

---

[1] Schwartz, B. (2015). *Why We Work*. Simon & Schuster: London.

environment at work has always played a large part in employee motivation and performance – what was once coined people's need for 'affiliation'. What I sometimes marvel at is how often these very basic motivation theories from decades ago are ignored, or at best re-hashed into the latest HR intervention.

We have known for decades that people aren't motivated by money, we know that people perform best in cohesive groups with shared goals, and that performance will depend on an individual's skills and motivation, balanced with the opportunity and support provided by the job role. However, we continue to offer pay as a reward, we monitor and control performance and we put people in work environments where they can barely survive, let alone thrive. The alternative would require a complete overhaul of practices, of doing things differently in HR, and seeking actual evidence for why we might embed a particular norm or practice in the organisation. For example, research by Alison Hirst from Angela Ruskin University[2] suggests that hotdesking (the practice of being asked to sit anywhere at work, rather than having a designated desk) is linked to higher workplace stress for 'hot-deskers' than control groups. Now, I haven't stringently reviewed this research, but it would question why we continue to see open-plan offices with 'agile' people jumping around hot-desks as progressive. At the very least, it should make us ask the question. This is what behavioural science can do for HR: the research itself is like the icing on the cake, but what is underpinning it; the foundations of curiosity, of asking the right question, and of applying this evidence to how we practise our work are like fairy dust for the

---

[2] Hirst, A. (2011). 'Settlers, vagrants and mutual indifference: Unintended consequences of hot-desking'. *Journal of Organizational Change Management*, Vol. 24, No. 6, pp. 767–782.

HR profession. We don't do this because it's so much easier to pay for the latest fad, and so much more interesting to try out the latest tool or survey on the market. It's also so much easier to continue 'as is'.

Our burning platform for change

But there's a burning platform for change. People are becoming savvy to the fact there is another way, and old HR practices just won't cut the mustard any longer. In the 1980s, teams cropped up called 'Human Capital' and it was all the rage to consider people as 'assets' and to spout about people being our 'strongest asset'. Let's not pretend it was all hugs, tea and sympathy at work before that, though. The industrial revolution marked the start of people working to time on a large scale, and great interest in people productivity. The divide between rich and poor, at least in the UK, was nothing to be proud of even back then. Though we started talking about people as assets decades later, what is clear is that people were still a commodity to be used to bring a profit to the organisation. What we are talking about here are human beings. The way we recruit someone into an organisation, the experience they have at work, and the stories and experience they take home to share with family and friends, is all part of their life. Organisations are a key part of the fabric of society and our human existence, and there is an enormous, somewhat daunting, opportunity here to do something differently. People want to work for organisations where they can find meaning in their work – if they are performing manual work, there are still massive opportunities for this work to be meaningful through social connection, the outcome of their work and their contribution to what the organisation achieves.

I spent the first few years of my career being told that I was 'too nice to be in HR'. They were picking up on the fact that I have a genuine and deeply felt care for people and their experience at work, and to be fair on occasion the heart on my sleeve did become emblazoned across my face and throughout my emails. However, the reason I first jumped ship from a generalist HR role was not because I was 'too nice', it was because I had a deep dislike for policy, process and rule books, aka HR manuals. I love a plan and parameters, but as a rule I only follow rules that I value, though luckily, I also value being a good citizen and staying out of jail. I like to understand how policies and process make a difference, and ultimately how they support whatever the organisation exists to achieve. I have studied human behaviour for as long as I can remember. I loved reading as a child because I loved getting under the skin of the character's emotional reactions, and the human dynamics unfurling on the page. I loved writing because it enabled me to create my own personalities on a page. And then I found psychology. I am a bona fide geek, and proud of it. I love science, I love the study of human behaviour and, moreover, I love the impact that applying this knowledge can have on people, relationships and work. And then I found Organisation Development (OD) almost by accident. Apparently, I was one of those people 'doing OD' who had absolutely no idea. I was busy learning about systems theory and change, and the wonders of organisational norms or ways of working, and I stumbled upon a field of practice that sought to improve organisational performance through applying learning from behavioural science. Whilst I devoured as many workshops and readings by the 'greats' in OD that I could, with particular devotion to Ed Schein and Mee-Yan Cheung-Judge amongst others, it left me feeling adrift from Human Resources and unsure how I could bridge that gap.

Applying learning from behavioural science to HR

In recent years, there have been efforts to apply the learnings from behavioural science into Human Resources, though I know from my days of carrying the title 'Occupational Psychologist' that the investment in employing people with deep subject matter expertise is still thin on the ground. Organisation Development is now a core capability for the HR profession, as proposed by the Chartered Institute for Personnel & Development, and there are a growing number of conferences and talks on the topic for HR professionals to benefit from. However, I think it would be fair to say that OD remains a somewhat elusive concept for many HR professionals. Whilst the larger organisations, and often corporations, invest heavily in OD, often with a core change management responsibility, smaller organisations and those more strapped for cash are likely to know little on the topic. And should they wish to venture into the world of OD, they would be faced with a manual or educational text. Unfortunately, this book isn't going to completely bridge that gap. I'm not aiming to write a seminal text on Behavioural Science for HR professionals. There are people far better qualified than I to do the job. I do, however, want to give it a shot – I'd like to share the magic of OD and how it can be part of all we do in HR. This is with the purpose of showing how it can really be a central part of putting the human back into Human Resources.

OD has its roots in humanistic theories. Developed in the 1930s, it came from a central premise that organisations can only prosper through aligning the ways of working, capabilities and needs of their people with the vision of the organisation. It sought to show the importance of connections, and not of tinkering around with policies and processes that were out of sync with the overall needs and direction of the organisation. One of the key theories in OD is of systems theory, where the organisation is considered to be a system made up of key component parts, which interact with each other to produce an output, or outcome. Systems theory is an incredibly important concept in understanding why creating change in one aspect of the system will have an impact on the other components of the system, but that one change alone may not create the change or 'systemic change' the organisation was aiming for. OD is a field of practice in its own right, though it often sits within HR departments and is more recently viewed to be an 'HR capability'. This has the potential to reduce OD to be a 'skill' demonstrated by a person, potentially someone who understands systemic change, and can design and front a change programme. However, an OD practitioner is so much more than this.

HR needs to throw out the rule book and get 'human'

The field of Human Resources has got itself in a muddle over the last ten or so years. We've tried so hard to be seen as 'business partners' that we've almost forgotten our core role to support, develop and motivate the 'humans' in that business. In an effort to show our worth, we've designed new functions within HR with names such as 'employee engagement' and 'employee experience', all aiming to achieve innovative plans, and all pretty much drawing on the same psychological theories and practices we knew of at least 20 to 30 years ago. It's become a re-marketing game, and whilst we're busy focusing on who has managed to get the highest survey result this year, across the board it would appear that, globally, people have never been unhappier at work.

I conducted a small number of interviews (approximately 15) with HR Directors, consultants and leaders to support my research for this book. I started by talking to people about compassion at work, but it then became clear that people were seeing HR as detracting from a focus on compassion and care for people, rather than championing this. One leader, a leader who had worked at very senior levels within the military, noted that our focus on compassion can often be 'codified' at work. In HR, we support our line managers to understand what they can do, and what they can give, to an employee who requires support. We give X numbers of days of compassionate leave, but only if the person who died is a close member of the family. We might allow unpaid leave, but it's at the 'manager's discretion' and depends on how busy we all are. This he described as 'codifying compassion' – we are codifying or standardising how to demonstrate a human emotion, how to care for another human being with individual needs. This probably best sums up my current and very personal challenge with how Human Resources has been conducted in the past – lots of rules, procedures and processes under the auspice of 'fairness', which in real terms rarely feels fair to anyone. This person told me a story of a lady who worked for him who he built great trust with, and one of the core ways in which they built trust was him offering her compassion at a time when she needed it most – when one of her parents passed away.

And how do we bring the human back into Human Resources for companies on tight deadlines and tight margins, where every minute of a person's time at work is calculated as a cost? If you haven't read James Bloodworth's *Hired*,[3] then my goodness, please do. It's fabulous to throw awards at the companies who take their staff away for weekend retreats, and who throw free breakfast and hot yoga on for their staff over lunch, but what about the real-life human beings who clock-on every morning, get told how many minutes they can take for a break each four to five hours, and face a disciplinary if they go a minute over? What about the employees who work for minimum wage, barely making ends meet, and who are treated as little more

---

[3] Bloodworth, J. (2019). *Hired: Six Months Undercover in Low-Wage Britain*. Atlantic Books: UK.

than a commodity? Surely if we're going to celebrate 'employee experience' as an HR profession, we should shine some enormous beacon on these practices? How can that honestly be the only way to achieve organisational performance and growth? And, when does anyone have a lightbulb moment when they question whether the moral imperative should trump profit when you're literally timing someone's toilet break, so their personal productivity doesn't lower? Now, admittedly, whilst I've worked across sectors, I've worked mainly in office environments, visiting pretty brilliant care centres, retail stores and professional services offices. I've seen varying work environments – from crumbling military accommodation, to spectacular stately homes used as offices, to the great heights of Canary Wharf and its endless escalators. I've also personally worked in a call centre though, and I lasted four days. I worked in a supermarket, where I lasted longer, and where we had to walk down onto the shop floor to a sign reading 'You're going on stage. Don't forget to smile.' We were usually too hungover to smile – I was 19 and worked in the café there to hang out with my friends, often eating 'traffic-light jellies' on the kitchen floor during breaks. I worked as a chambermaid, a silver service waitress, in endless temp jobs in factories and warehouses, and my own highlight – processing photos in 'Snappy Snaps'. In none of these many jobs did I have any inkling of an HR department, beyond the fact that someone paid me, and I received a payslip. My first real experience of an HR department was when I lost my first graduate job as a corporate tax consultant before it even started and ended up applying for an HR graduate scheme for a law firm. It was a brilliant scheme, working with some excellent HR folk, but my own early beginnings in HR were quite adrift from anything I'd personally experienced as an employee. So what? I wonder how far HR has come to matter to everyone, to all businesses, and to be progressive in all businesses. Or whether it remains the remit of the companies with the big bucks, or where they are just fortunate to have a very forward-thinking executive team and/or HR Leader. There are call centres, care centres and small businesses with simply stunning HR practices. And then there are large-scale corporations hiring thousands of people that treat them akin to paperclips.

Turning the tides together

My purpose in writing this book is not to take a dig at capitalism. That would be somewhat rich, as I spent my early career working for large global corporates, though riches sadly never fell into my lap. However, I do think there is an opportunity for all to use this book to learn more about how behavioural science, and specifically OD, can support our practice as HR professionals, and to bring the human back into HR. And I do think there is an even bigger opportunity for us to do the right thing – to challenge where we see or know this isn't the case within our profession, and to use our collective voice to bring change. Yes, let's make sure we've got our own house in order first, fair enough. But let's work together as an HR and OD professional to bring societal change where people are treated like people, and not paperclips.

There can be a tendency within HR to lean on short-term interventions. This is perhaps born out of an economic and business context where 'busyness' is celebrated, and everything needed to be done yesterday. The 'time is money' mantra has done us no favours there and suggests that expediency should take favour over quality of outcome. Within HR, far more often than not, these interventions are both sensible and very well-intended. For example, well-being programmes. I am a huge advocate of supporting people's mental health, both positive well-being and raising awareness of mental health issues. However, evidence suggests that these well-being programmes have limited impact on employee engagement or indeed on workplace productivity. This doesn't matter greatly if the investment has been made on moral and 'human' grounds, but sadly we often hear organisations suggesting the enormous return on investment in monetary terms of their well-being programmes. Whilst it might be true that employee absence is costing the economy £x billion per annum, it is also somewhat far-fetched that a programme of well-being workshops, and getting employees to exercise more and eat healthily, is going to be the panacea that gets them out of bed and whistling as they work. And this is where OD comes in. What systemic change needs to be brought about to create a shift in employee absence? And what burning question, what well-thought out hypothesis are we trying to test here? This is where HR falls down repeatedly – whilst we talk about building OD capability, a central part of HR training does not focus on the curiosity of thought, the analytical thinking, the hypothesis building and research skills that would support people to hone their craft in the field.

A guide to navigating this book

This book is ordered into four key sections:

1. Section one: Shaping the future of HR
   This section will introduce the concept that someone or something has taken the 'human' out of Human Resources, and I propose that we need to re-humanise the world of work and need to put that 'human' back in place within our HR functions. As an introduction to two key tenets of achieving this, I then take you on a whistle-stop tour of motivation theories and why free fruit and a table tennis table isn't going to truly win your people over. The second key tenet of putting the 'human' back into Human Resources is via evidence-based practice, or actually testing a few well-thought-out

hypotheses, as opposed to just trying on a few new fads that might be the next big thing in employee engagement. What you'll find in practice is that, having shared quite a few stories and quite a bit of anecdotal 'evidence', I put forward an argument for doing it all properly and taking on board evidence-based practice in HR. If that doesn't infuriate you enough to close the book, you'll move onto Section two.

2. Section two: Creating a people-focused culture
   The purpose of putting the 'human' back into Human Resources is to prevent people from being treated like paperclips in organisations across the globe. We'll explore whether we can manage or can't manage change, and how we can influence and shape organisational culture. The section will bring in thinking from the world of OD and behavioural science, and we will delve into systems thinking as a model and a mechanism for creating sustainable change and for creating cultures that care for their people. The final chapter of this section is devoted to a topic close to my heart, 'compassion at work'. If we are to drive people-focused cultures and practices through all we achieve in HR, we need to have an awareness and understanding of what 'compassion' and 'empathy' look like in ways of working, behaviours and leadership practices.

3. Section three: Leading an HR service with heart
   This is arguably the most practical section because it relates specifically to what you can do, and what you can develop and build in your own team. It's easier to influence than building a case for systemic change, but no less important. We'll consider how to rebrand your team, if needed, and I will be sharing ideas and tips for putting the 'human' back into your own HR professional practice and into our people processes and policies. We will focus on re-humanising the

world of work through the seemingly small-scale stuff that actually has a large impact. For example, take the simple induction programme for a new starter. An induction experience lacking in personalised care and attention will be remembered by new starters and may have a lasting impact on how connected and loyal they are to the organisation.

4. Section four: Over to you
    It is here that we draw together some of the key themes of the book, and I ask you to consider all that you can do to re-humanise your workplace and to support others to do the same. I am passionate that work is about treating people like 'people not paperclips', and that our current people processes, practices and ways of working serve to cause or at least to exacerbate this. This section is a call to action for you to actively shake up the system with me, to be a fellow change agent with a 'people not paperclips' plan.

Each of the sections outlined above will be broken down into a series of relevant chapters, which will share a mix of research, stories and sometimes just my own viewpoint. There will be a summary at the end of each chapter to support you in making the connection to what comes next. Each section can stand alone, so do dip in and out as needed. There will also be a toolkit at the end of each chapter or topic area, and this is to bring a more practical element into the book. It might just be a series of questions to reflect on having read the chapter or may be a set of proposed actions you could take to apply the research and thinking within your own organisation. Not all of these toolkits will feel relevant to you, but I would suggest you stay curious and try to give them a whirl.

I've already introduced myself and why I am writing this book; why now and why me. In terms of my style, you are likely to find it very informal. I am seeking to bring forward some big topics in an accessible and interesting way. Whilst this is a business book, I hope your experience of reading it will feel more like having a catch up over a coffee than listening to a speech in a business conference or lecture theatre. If nothing else, I've sought to retain my authentic voice throughout this book, which at times will slip into an informality. I've spent most of this book-writing process knee-deep in imposter syndrome, but I want to take this opportunity just to remind myself and you as a reader that any informality, storytelling or viewpoint-sharing should not be perceived as a lack of knowledge. It's there, I promise you, but I chose to write a book that I hope you will be able to read on a commute to work, rather than assign to the dusty 'textbook' shelf. I'm a Chartered Occupational Psychologist, Senior HR Professional, a Fellow of the Chartered Institute of Personnel & Development and a Certified Executive Coach. However, the most important thing I bring to this book is my deep faith in humanity and the role that compassion can play in our experience of the workplace. We in HR can play a huge part in the future of work. We're people, not paperclips.

SECTION ONE

SHAPING THE FUTURE OF HUMAN RESOURCES

Chapter 1

What really does motivate people?

Introduction

In this chapter, we will explore why people may not report being 'happy' or 'engaged' at work, and we will draw on thinking from behavioural science to determine what might actually motivate our people. We will discuss the concept of 'meaning' at work; what is it, and where can we all get some? And we'll touch on the ever-debated topic of money as a motivator. The toolkit in this chapter is there to support you in exploring what motivates your people (your employees, or perhaps your own team, or further still, yourself). This is a hugely broad topic that is central to how we build people-focused cultures and put the human back into our HR plans.

Drawing on behavioural science to respond to our 'global epidemic' of disengagement

Apparently, we're operating within a 'global epidemic' of workplace disengagement (Gallup, 2018). It all sounds pretty awful. Where do we go next? We've been investing in 'employee engagement' interventions for at least a couple of decades, and nothing much seems to have shifted. If we're trying to create sustainable change in our workplaces, and I'm assuming that's the end game, I'm still pondering to myself, 'What is engagement?'

and ultimately, 'How is it going to help us to achieve that?' 'Do we need to go back to the drawing board, and ultimately back to the evidence?'

Employee engagement is nothing new. And so much of it is based on shaky evidence. If we're pondering 'where next?', I wonder if we should look to a couple of fields that have existed all along. It could be that drawing on existing and refined tools and models from the world of occupational psychology could support how we 'engage' and motivate our people? There's a difference between seeing employee engagement as a programme of interventions and seeing it as a long-term outcome built through a deep understanding of the needs and motivation of real people. To pretend we can create 'business success' on the basis of employee engagement interventions such as responding to a survey at a snapshot in time, or through free fruit and table tennis tables, is, quite frankly, bonkers. I would suggest we need to slow down, stop over-egging our interventions, and reflect on the evidence out there.

So, what factors might create meaning in the workplace?

Many years of 'climate surveys', providing a snapshot of employee feedback or 'mood', suggest that line managers, and probably also the HR teams, so often fail to understand what will retain and what will cause an employee to leave an organisation. Tony Schwartz (2016)[4] suggests that satisfied people who report finding meaning in their work typically also report feeling 'in charge'. Schwartz noted that satisfied people he observed achieved a

---

[4] Schwartz, T. (2016). *The Way We're Working Isn't Working.* Simon & Schuster: UK.

measure of autonomy and discretion at work, and they used that autonomy and discretion to achieve a level of expertise. They learned new things, developing both as employees and as people, and they experienced what Schwartz termed 'growth'.

When asked what motivates them at work, employees reliably answer the same things, in generally the same order. When managers are asked what they think motivates employees, they too generally answer consistently, but just with completely different items.

The key engagement factors, often cited by employees:

1. *Appreciation of work done* – a simple thank you or recognition for their contribution. Our reaction to this in HR has been to build systems that can pop a thank you to people on email. I'm far from being a luddite, but I do find it interesting how we are just itching to depersonalise what could just be a simple human connection with a few simple words thrown in.

2. *Being involved and influencing how work is done* – another one that makes perfect sense but is missing in many work environments. I've witnessed this lack of involvement many times and it is particularly prevalent in middle management, where managers may feel disconnected from strategy development or planning but be expected to 'do' what is set by others.

3. *The organisation extending care and loyalty* – we can codify compassion into HR policies, but ultimately what really engages employees is their line managers and colleagues responding to their individual, personal and emotional needs when it really matters. Showing empathy and compassion is what makes us human, and is the basis of healthy human relationships, so why would we expect any of the factors that sit below to come before it?

Key engagement factors, as very often envisaged by line managers and HR professionals:

1. *Pay* – in the eyes of many organisations, engagement rests solely on a cost of living salary increase, with occasional 'rewards' for good behaviour.

2. *Job security* – that old adage: 'as long as we don't sack them/ make them redundant, they're singing on their way to work.' Unlikely.

3. *Promotion* – the pathways to promotion are often unclear or misunderstood in organisations. It should be a relief to us all then that this isn't the top motivator for employees.

We often plan our engagement interventions in response to the three priorities above, and often therefore really miss the mark. What else motivates our employees?

Opportunities to grow

Whilst having 'a great team' around you might motivate you to work even harder, opportunities to grow and develop are often cited as being reasons for employees to remain in an organisation. According to a BambooHR survey of more than 1,000 workers, a lack of opportunities is the largest contributor to people starting to seek those opportunities elsewhere. This seems obvious, and the very reason of course that we invest in learning and development and talent interventions. However, how far do we tailor discussions to the individual? How far do we create meaningful career discussions that link where someone wants to be, to where they are now and consider motivating and potentially exciting opportunities to bridge that gap or to take the aspiration even further? Do our HR processes facilitate a meaningful conversation for each employee, or do they facilitate a tick box exercise to complete a process, or worse still simply to produce a rating to pop into a spreadsheet?

Engaging, interesting work

Employee engagement and job satisfaction are not the same thing. An employee can love his or her job, have fantastic pay and colleagues, whilst still dragging themselves into work every day to do a job they find painfully dull. I exaggerate, but we all know someone who stayed in a job far too long because they say they 'really liked the people'… until that just wasn't enough anymore. When we're creating HR processes and ways of working that foster meaningful conversations for employees, we need to ensure these conversations explore how that person can engage further with their work. How do we focus on enhancing meaning in the present, and not just looking forward to a 'career plan' for the future? It's wonderful to have a five-year plan mapped out, but ever-deferred engagement doesn't help anyone to feel happy at work. This is where creative job design, stretch assignments or stretch objectives, fostering innovation and creativity in the workplace and encouraging flexibility beyond the 'bum on a seat' needs to be parked in yesteryear.

The search for meaning at work, and the link to social contact and control

So how can we find greater meaning at work, and why does this matter to us in HR? Like other fields, HR professionals often seek new shiny objects (ideas) that will help people to perform better. For these new insights to shift from distractions to sustainable, value-added practices, they need to be examined more rigorously. Spending time exploring the evidence-base for an intervention, particularly when it's new and shiny so doesn't have one yet, is often placed into the 'too hard box' by HR practitioners. I've certainly been guilty of this in the past, perhaps because the intervention just seems so obviously positive. How could it possibly fail to increase people's job satisfaction? However, spending time upfront defining your hypothesis, or rather what you're trying to affect or explore, based on hopefully at least a bit of an understanding of the current evidence-base, will stand us all in good stead to avoid spending a lot of time and money on quick fixes that fix very little.

We've established that people are searching for meaning; a search for meaning in life in general, but this applies just as much to the workplace. If we are all hankering after meaning in our work, why have so many people got jobs where, quite frankly, pay is the only real motivator for showing up? Pay, or the fear of not receiving any pay, of course. Try as they might to find meaning, challenge and room for autonomy, this work situation often leaves them looking for just the bare basics of a salary. Gallup research, which some rate and some question for its reliability, has found that 90% of people surveyed spend half their waking lives doing things they would rather not be doing at places they would rather not be; they're working in jobs they despise, or at best tolerate. I've been challenged on this topic a few times when discussing how we can create meaning and social connection in all organisations. One challenge came from an old colleague who asked me: 'How on earth can you think people packing sanitary towels in a factory are searching for meaning from their work?' You'll see I haven't abridged the question for you. I really can think that, and I do, and it's based on a whole host of research on the importance of social connection. For a full deep-dive into the topic, please refer to fantastic books in social psychology such as *The Social Animal*, by Elliot Aronson.[5]

---

[5] Aronson, E. (2003). *The Social Animal*, revised ed. Worth Publishing: Duffield, UK.

For a more anecdotal approach from me, please read on. And please note that I don't share my stories as 'pseudo-evidence'. They are stories to illustrate my own experience, and often in an attempt to bring the research I am citing to life a little for you. Our next chapter focuses on evidence-based practice in HR, and the irony of this is not lost on me.

So, how does engagement and job satisfaction apply to people who aren't in typical high-flying careers, or what in the United Kingdom at least were once known as 'white collar jobs'? I worked as a chambermaid cleaning up sick, owl poo (yes, somehow this is true) and goodness knows what else at the weekend and during holidays before starting university. I was, broadly speaking, motivated in that role. It wasn't just the money; I wasn't rolling in it as a sixteen-year-old chambermaid. The camaraderie and the laughter amongst the chambermaids, the porters and the people in the laundry was brilliant. It was hard work in every sense, but I got up after sometimes two hours' sleep from a night of dancing to carry hefty hoovers up and down flights of stairs at 8 am. I was engaged. Or I was when I wasn't hiding in cleaning cupboards eating leftover pastries. (How did I end up in HR? Goodness knows.) Meaning at work comes from a wide range of factors, but we can tap into this and make virtually any workplace more engaging and more 'human' for our people. Why do I now labour this point? I value fairness and compassion above all else, and I have a strong 'elitism radar'. I don't want to write a book that seeks to bring humanity into only the head offices of the richest companies in the world, though goodness they need it, and if I'm honest I miss working somewhere with a swimming pool in the building. This is, and should be, for everyone. I'm not so naïve to think that people working in unsafe factories on less than the legal national minimum wage work for people who are about to pick up this book. We have another fight to fight for those people, and it's beyond the realms of this book. We need to put the human back into HR for these people. It's not all about the people who get free food in swanky offices – we're designing the future of work for all, and these people sadly aren't the majority.

So, what does motivate people and what can we learn from this in HR? The behavioural economist, Dan Ariely,[6] has said that 'when we think about how people work, the naïve intuition we have is that people are like rats in a maze'. In line with the motivation theories of the greats such as Maslow,[7] Ariely conducted research in 2008 that found we are motivated by far more than money and comfort incentives, such as free fruit, or even by the offer of working and being paid for less hours through flexible working. We are driven by the meaning found in our work, by the support and acknowledgement of others and, interestingly, also by how challenging the task is. Ariely found that the harder the task is, the prouder we are in achieving this, and this research supports my point above that people are complex creatures and our motivations for joining a company, performing well there and then choosing to stay can be wide-ranging and complex. I have shared feeling motivated and potentially 'happy' as a chambermaid. This could have been because it was only a couple of days a week at most and represented disposable income rather than my life's work. I don't know. I certainly didn't feel the same job satisfaction in my foray as a call centre worker. I lasted four days, four long days, before calling the agency and saying I couldn't go back. The crunch factor for me wasn't even clocking on or off the phones to go

---

[6] Ariely, D. (2008). *Predictably Irrational: The Hidden Forces that Shape Our Decisions*. HarperCollinsPublishers Ltd: London.

[7] Maslow, A. H. (18 July 2013) [first published 1968]. *Toward a Psychology of Being*. Simon & Schuster: New York.

to the toilet (and having this logged as a 'statistic', rather than a pretty basic human function), or the fact that I was trying to sell some phone-related gadget to people who neither wanted nor needed it. No, the crunch factor was watching our statistics put on the whiteboard and our Call Centre Manager jumping up and down when someone exceeded their targets. I honestly couldn't have cared less. There was zero meaning in that role for me, and zero social contact to bolster the lack of meaning in the activities themselves. Social exchanges were precisely timed, and actively discouraged. I know call centre environments have moved on greatly in 20 years, but back then they were the battery farms of the workplace. Twenty-eight long hours. And please bear in mind that I managed to find joy cleaning up after people in an expensive hotel, serving food in a Chinese restaurant on a wage of next-to-nothing and developing endless photos in a shop. Social contact and an element of control – this shouldn't be the rocket science of effective job design.

Revisiting the impact of pay on how we motivate our people

Can money be a strong motivator? We know that money is a 'hygiene factor'; not enough and we feel demotivated, but increasing amounts will not result in ever-increasing happiness. However, Ariely, who I introduced a moment ago, has found in controlled laboratory experiments that the less appreciated we feel our work is, the more money we want to be paid to do it. So of course, as always suspected, money matters a great deal to people – however, it is the value it represents on our worth that makes a difference here. This is why paying people equitably, when they've performed well, or their role has grown significantly, really matters. It's not the numbers on the payslip, it's the value you are placing on their worth at work. I will share a specific example with you. Ariely conducted a study, published in *Psychological Science*,[8] where he gave students at MIT a piece of paper filled with random letters and asked them to find the pairs of identical letters on the paper. Each time they did the activity, they were offered less money than the previous time to play. Those in the first group wrote their names on their sheets and handed them to the experimenter, who simply said 'Uh huh' before putting it in a pile. People in the second group didn't write down their names, and the experimenter put their sheets in a pile without looking at them. People in the third group had their work shredded immediately upon completion. What did they find? People whose work was shredded needed twice as much money as those whose work was acknowledged in order to keep doing the task. People in the second group, whose work was saved but ignored, needed almost as much money as those whose work was shredded. Ariely demonstrated the sizeable impact that ignoring people's contribution and effort can have on their motivation, and this has been supported in numerous studies since. Of course, we may overinflate just how valuable our own work is, and no one wants to be average. However, it seems very clear that acknowledging the contribution and performance of a person is a basic motivational need, and one which really shouldn't be so hard to achieve or to facilitate in HR.

Taking steps to tailor reward and recognition to individual needs

What steps can we take to move beyond the obvious yet ineffectual motivators to tailor our offering to the needs of our

---

[8] Heyman, J. and Ariely, D. (2004). 'Effort for payment: A tale of two markets'. *Psychological Science*, Vol. 15, No. 11, pp. 787–793.

people? There will be many, and the answer to that question is probably a book in itself. I will share below some small nudges that will move us in the right direction.

- Consider how you can build a *feedback culture* within your organisation. This doesn't need to be attached to a big marketing campaign or a training programme. Tell people why it's important, help them to understand what good looks like through role-modelling, and reinforce it through acknowledging them when they do it. Start in the HR department, and then share your success stories and learnings with others.

- *Acknowledge, appreciate and recognise people, role-modelling this within your own team* when people are doing more than expected, or when they're taking on more responsibility. We don't typically have endless money to give discretionary pay increases, and it wouldn't necessarily be fair of HR to encourage such practices, but valuing others' contribution is even more important than attaching a financial incentive to that. Remember the research I just shared stating when people feel undervalued, they may want to be paid more as a result? This is important stuff.

- *Ask people.* Engagement surveys serve a useful purpose within organisations. They are a feedback mechanism that provides a snapshot in time, or sometimes real-time feedback, for how a person is experiencing their team 'climate'. Engagement surveys are not a measure of organisational culture, but it never fails to surprise me just how far some HR teams are willing to go to extrapolate the results and to suggest cultural change is underpinned by their 30–40 question employee survey. It's just a survey. Absolutely use the data to inform your next steps but get out there and speak to people. Ask people what motivates them, explore their values and how closely the organisation is meeting their needs.

The number of articles and books on happiness at work has grown sizably over recent years. There is something that feels so obviously good about chasing the elusive 'happiness at work', or perhaps something so obviously bad about saying we shouldn't do so. Isn't it obvious that we should feel happiness at work? Isn't that what the term 'work-life blend' was created for? Happiness has been the gold at the end of the rainbow for some time in business journals, but it appears that happiness may just be a symptom of something much more important – meaning. Whilst happiness and meaning are related, it isn't always the case that the high presence of one should signal the high presence of the other. Findings from the work of Rd. Barbara Fredrickson at the University of North Carolina examined self-reported levels of happiness and meaning, and found that 75% of people reported high scores on levels of happiness, but low on levels of meaning. Further research has found that employees who find meaning in their work are three times more likely to stay with their organisations than those who don't find meaning in their work. We're back to one of the basic premises of motivation theory. It's important to reiterate my earlier point though: it's not all about finding meaning from the incredible impact you're achieving at work. Whilst pay is certainly not a core motivator, some people can only find meaning from their pay and how they can use that pay to support or to stay afloat in their personal life. It would be a pretty romantic notion to pretend that this doesn't matter, and anyone who isn't living 'hand to mouth', as we say in the UK, in a time of high austerity, is very fortunate. That said, our focus should always be on bringing everyone up, and for HR this should mean bringing everyone up to a way of working that has dignity, fulfils social needs and seeks to be motivating.

Summary

This chapter has been an introduction or indeed a reminder to what motivates people, and what has some potential to motivate but is never going to be the silver bullet, that is, money. I have no doubt you knew much of this. The reason I've kicked off a book about putting the 'human' back into Human Resources with a chapter about human motivation despite knowing that this is 'nothing new' is that we often forget that humans have wide-ranging needs and motivations. If it's not new, it's still not practised in organisations. We've made some headway through designing flexible benefits schemes and in designing workplaces to support social contact and collaboration, but the majority of organisations still exist in hierarchies with limited delegated authorities between the layers or even open communication and involvement. As a profession, Human Resources can play a huge role in re-examining and re-communicating the 'person case' for ensuring our processes, practices and ways of working facilitate social contact, empowerment, autonomy and control where achievable, and an approach tailored to the needs of individuals.

The next chapter will explore how we define and test the strategies and interventions that will create person-centred workplaces where people can do their best work. We will discuss the importance of gathering evidence to make informed decisions for how we develop and shape our HR strategies and plans. We would never make a business decision, or shouldn't, without looking at objective fact and logic. So, why do we chase after the latest fad when it comes to people management and development? Why are we still relying on 'engagement surveys' and performance management systems that fail to increase anything other than frustration in many organisations? I'm endlessly inspired by behavioural science and by research that seeks to understand human behaviour so that we can apply this to make our workplaces more effective for all. You and I don't need to spend our lives thinking up and conducting this research, but my goodness what a missed opportunity if we don't even know it's there or take the time to explore it. I'm a bona fide geek and proud of it. I will be delighted if you read the next chapter and it ignites your 'inner geek' a little.

Toolkit A: Engaging your people

1. *Explore your purpose or intent*

   ○ *Consider why you're focusing on what motivates your people.* Bear with me here. It may seem bleedingly obvious but defining your purpose will guide where you focus your attention when we move to information gathering. Is this because it is a general expectation of the HR department? Is it because the market is competitive in terms of finding or retaining talented people? Is it because your senior leadership want to be known for creating a culture where people are valued and respected? Whatever it is, note it down.

   ○ *Test and agree your purpose with others.* Is this what you should be aiming for, or prioritising, as a business at the moment? Defining and agreeing on this matters: when you go out to speak to people, which we'll come onto next, this will be how you introduce your curiosity. You're defining it at this stage because people have exceptionally strong BS detectors and it helps to be able to share your intent honestly and openly with them. If the honest answer is that no one other than you cares, but you're delving into this to build that person case, that's absolutely fine too (or it is for the purpose of this task).

---

2. *Develop and test your understanding of your people – what motivates them?*

   ○ *Ask them.* Spend time *speaking with your people*, your business leaders and HR colleagues to understand what motivates differing groups of people in your organisation. Talk to real people, people you wouldn't usually connect with, at this stage. If you think you've done this, stay curious and see what else you can find out.

   ○ *Listen and apply professional curiosity.* Do you observe and hear differing needs and motivations depending on professional groupings, personal demographics or office location? How do you know this?

   ○ *Delve deeper.* Consider *other engagement data* you have to draw on – climate surveys, team feedback, leavers' interviews, ad hoc feedback and feedback or issues raised through employee relations cases. What do these tell you about people's needs and how they are or are not being met?

   ○ *Look for patterns and themes with someone else.* Consider the patterns and themes you find across both the quantitative and qualitative data you've gathered. Show it to another trusted person, in confidence naturally, and ask them what they see. You're trying to explore the less obvious points – what does someone see from the 'outside in'?

3. *Sense-making and prioritisation*

   ○ *Start to make sense of what you've found.* You've defined why exploring what motivates your own people matters, and you've explored this yourself and with others. You'll have hopefully found out some really interesting information or refuted/supported what you thought you already knew. Fantastic. And, 'so what'? It's now time for synthesising your information and some sense-making. I love this stage. It's creative and allows you to consider practical steps for making your people feel valued, respected and motivated at work.

○ *Isolate your 'engagement priorities'* or the differences that will make a difference to how you motivate your people. For example, you want to retain people because you have a high turnover rate and it's disruptive and expensive. Your people are motivated by being involved in decisions that matter to them, they want to use their professional expertise to create impact, and certain teams are motivated by the opportunity to innovate and to develop their external profile. Great. But none of this happens. You've isolated your engagement priorities.

4. *In deciding your interventions, keep it simple. A few tips.*

○ Ask real people for their opinions. You're not Netflix or whoever else, so don't build your engagement interventions based on somebody else's slide deck. Refer to others' ideas for inspiration but ask real-life people wandering around your offices what they would like to see.

○ Remember technology is an enabler, not the 'solution'. There are many tools available to support us to communicate better at work. In the same way that clicking a 'like' thumbs-up button on social media isn't the same as actually taking meaningful social action, an employee communication mechanism that isn't mirrored in open communication within the organisation will have limited impact. Technology enables cultural change, but your purpose needs to be achieved through careful consideration of how you can adapt your processes, ways of working, and most importantly, how your leadership can lead the way.

○ You've gathered information and translated it into possibilities. This now needs to be owned and led by your leaders. Engagement and motivation aren't an HR issue – as we know, it's a business issue and therefore needs to be led by your leaders.

Chapter 2

Creating impact through evidence-based practice and innovation

Introduction

Having explored what motivates people and why it matters, we could be tempted to want to run off and change the world before breakfast. This chapter is an opportunity to step back and to reflect on how we might achieve that – in effect, a brief pause before we do in fact run off and change the world together. We will explore two key areas of work that will support us to create greater impact as HR functions. We want to create greater impact so that we shift our organisations toward being genuinely people-focused, but the topics we'll explore will support you in achieving impact for any purpose. We will be exploring evidence-based practice in the workplace, and innovation as a skill, a value and a mechanism for change.

I will share the benefits of adopting 'evidence-based practice' in our work and will show how this need not be an onerous pursuit but has the potential to support better decision-making. I will raise awareness of the limitations of the beloved case study as a potential 'evidence-base', that is, 'but it worked for them…'. And last, we'll explore the role that innovation can and should play in driving our impact as an HR function. Innovation stretches the realms of what is possible in an organisation or for an individual, and a lack of innovation is what keeps some HR functions lagging behind as 'personnel departments' of yesteryear.

Introducing evidence-based practice as a no-brainer for the HR function

Decisions that can affect people and organisational decisions should not be based on guesswork or less than accurate data. We might invest a fortune in certain employee benefits or in employee bonuses, with no research to support these other than a ten-minute TED Talk and a brief Google search. So, we need to base our decisions on accurate data that we understand and need to ensure our decisions are also based on wider evidence. There are rarely silver bullets to solve our organisational problems, and however tempting it may be to rely on a shiny TED Talk or conference session to guide a 'quick fix', it will take a little more time and research to get to the right answer. This is where 'evidence-based practice' or seeking evidence to support our decisions, activities and interventions in Human Resources is hugely important to achieving any meaningful change.

The Key Performance Indicator (KPI) – we love it in HR, even if we're not always sure of what we're measuring, or perhaps why we're doing so. I'm going to propose in this chapter that we in HR would benefit from stepping away from our scorecard, or management report, and taking some time to reflect on why we're collecting this information. Or perhaps reflecting on how reliable or valid that data is; is it accurate, is it replicable and is it even measuring what we think it is? Many HR departments are hugely adept at HR analytics and rely on this data, and the data trends it supports, to inform their decision-making. As ever, it's wonderful when it goes well or when people are doing it well, but I would suggest the majority of busy and potentially under-resourced HR departments continue to manually tot up their staff turnover, and not a great deal else, on an Excel spreadsheet, not quite knowing what any of the data is telling them. I share this because I've worked in enough of these departments and I won't pretend that I swanned in and improved the situation.

Let me share a couple of recent examples to illustrate the importance of conducting evidence-based practice. Following an allegedly racially biased incident at one of their US stores, a large coffee chain promptly invested in a swathe of unconscious bias-training workshops for their staff. Was there time to consider if such workshops actually create behavioural change, and more so the behavioural change they were seeking? Probably not. Even when not faced with a large-scale PR issue, we readily move to 'doing stuff'. If we're paying for it, and someone is doing something, it's got to be good. It reminds me of that old adage for beginner joggers, when they have a squeaky-clean gym kit but no concept of a training plan: 'All the gear, but no idea.' I'm not being unkind, I've been there. It's also so easy to pick up the next exciting fad, in an effort to look cutting-edge. Cutting-edge needs to be more closely aligned to impact than idea for me. It's quick and easy enough to access a range of attractive HR 'solutions' via a quick Google of our issue or problem or giving a call to any available external consultant. But there is something vital and also quite refreshing about putting Google aside for a moment and considering how we can support our decision-making minus all the fads, trends and cognitive biases on offer via an internet search. Whilst we bring our HR expertise into play to inform the final decision, regardless of the pull of the Google search results, ensuring we consider and conduct an exploration of the evidence-base for any HR solutions we find.

Another example could be introducing a new performance-related pay (PRP) framework for an organisation. This is a time-consuming investment, and ultimately the model requires financial and emotional investment from the organisation. An HR professional would want to research and understand, 'How far does PRP increase individual and organisational performance at work?' Whilst there will not be a definitive answer, I can promise you that the pursuit of the answer will provide a hugely interesting foray into the world of motivation at work and employee recognition. The pursuit of the answer, or even the pursuit of refining the question you want to ask, will give you access to networks, thinking and debates you would easily bypass through a so-called quick fix. I will say repeatedly in this book, there is no such thing as a 'quick fix', only a 'quick sticking plaster'. The danger of quick-fix solutions is they offer a distraction from continuing a deeper exploration of your answer. This chapter is going to introduce you to the notion of evidence-based practice, or perhaps to re-ignite or refresh your interest in the topic. For those who are expert in this topic, feel free to skip onto the next chapter. This chapter is intended as an introduction and to inspire curiosity – it's highly unlikely to excite anyone with deep knowledge in the field. It may in fact offend them. If this inspires you to draw on the sources that I cite alongside my introduction, I'll have my achieved my aim.

The case for evidence-based practice

The case is simple, and naturally evidence-based. Drawing on better quality evidence to inform our decision-making and testing the reliability and validity of that evidence in relation to the question we're seeking to explore, is quite clearly going to support more robust decision-making. It serves to cut out the host of biases we're all subject to as human beings and facilitates a thinking process that is more likely to achieve our desired outcomes.

I'll outline the case in bullet-format:

- more informed and effective decision-making for HR professionals;

- HR policy and practice will be based upon what works, rather than what it is hoped might work, representing a stronger investment of time and cost;

- more consistent decision-making and interventions, which inspire confidence in HR leadership;

- greater ability to align your HR practices with the strategic goals of your organisation;

- improved credibility for the discipline of human resource practice and for practitioners, thus leading to your stakeholders wanting to involve you in strategic decision-making;

- effective management of risk, based on reliable data sources.

It's all pretty impressive.

How can we embed evidence-based practice into Human Resources?

So, how can you start to consider and adopt evidence-based HR in your own professional practice? The Centre for Evidence-Based Management (CEBMa)[9] contains a wealth of resources to support you. From my own experience and drawing on the recommendations of others, including the CEBMa, I have detailed a few key pointers below:

---

[9] www.cebma.org

1. *Start out with an answerable question* – what is it that you are seeking evidence in response to? This is scientific enquiry, so naturally we want to start out with a hypothesis that has been considered and formed for a reason. So often we start out 'researching' or potentially 'googling' without a clear sense of what we are looking for, and why. I've certainly gone down a few rabbit holes myself with that approach.

2. *Explore the area* – don't just dive in. Scientific literature is important in helping us to think about new areas to question and helps give context and meaning to the organisational data we collate. I would love to encourage a literature review when commencing all new projects or exploring new interventions in HR. If this makes you feel exhausted just thinking about it, at least dive into the brilliant literature reviews and reports through organisations such as Science for Work,[10] which are committed to furthering evidence-based practice in organisations.

3. *Analyse the sources of your evidence* – this is where your critical thinking will come to the fore, a skill needed in spades in HR and luckily within evidence-based practice. When considering what evidence, we should pay attention to, we need to consider why we are paying attention to certain data above other sources, and to really question the validity of that data. Is the employee survey really measuring team engagement? Is the exit interview data really telling us why people are leaving? These seem obvious, but they really aren't. Consider how the data was collected, by whom, with what purpose, and how reliable and accurate that data really is.

---

[10] https://scienceforwork.com/

4. *Draw on a wide range of evidence to inform your thinking* – 'hard' data, for example, your employee turnover data, sickness absence rates, and other such 'people stuff' is really important, but it is not the only source of evidence. As an aside, why is it even called 'hard' data? I have the HR battle wounds to prove that the 'soft' data is often far more painful to collate and understand.

We read headlines about HR innovation and HR disruption, but then instead of robustly testing this, we just cut and paste a solution from another sector into our own organisation as if context wasn't a factor. We talk about HR as a strategic business partner, but how can we hope to achieve this if we don't develop a robust discipline surrounding evidence-based practice and applying rigour to our decision-making processes? My background is in occupational psychology and I've always found it interesting that, in HR, we talk about HR 'best practice' as if it is based on some form of scientific logic. 'Best practice' is often termed 'best' because others did it and they have achieved some form of success. Let's explore the use of case studies in building our evidence-based practice now.

The use of case studies as an 'evidence' base

We've established that HR has a bit of a way to go in embedding evidence-based practice within our profession. At present, the most relied upon source for HR decision-making is the aforementioned and much-loved case study. I've spent 20 years listening to case studies, many actually incredibly interesting and inspiring, and reading articles about the 'next big thing' based on what another organisation are doing. This is inspiring, it's interesting and it's a learning opportunity, but it's certainly not a route to shaping your own people strategy and practices. It's the chase for the unicorn – we're likely to end up with a donkey.[11] Case studies are often compelling stories. In any given context, the situation you face and your organisation faces is going to be unique, and your response to that will also be unique. No matter what you can read about another company or leader facing 'similar' challenges, it is virtually impossible to directly apply the actions taken to your own situation and to achieve the same results. If this were possible, we would all have read the infamous PowerPoint pack from Netflix and have the same culture as them by now. We were inspired, but I imagine few achieved any profound cultural shifts or even sought to do so after reading it.

Any business or team we hear about in a case study is operating as a system; an incredibly complex set of interrelated 'features' made up of people, processes and systems, both formal and informal. A case study can rarely capture exactly what is going on within such a complex system. We'll talk more about organisations as systems later in the book. For now, it's important to note that when an organisational system is in good health (financially prosperous, people are staying), it can seem that everything going on in that system is a causal factor for creating this positive picture, and vice versa. Successful companies tend to over-emphasise the leadership heroes who supported or support their success, or they ignore the sheer weight of luck in the success they've achieved. The organisation has done well, so all elements of the system are up for grabs as an example of how to achieve that same success. This is known as 'survivor bias'; the organisation or leader 'survived' or succeeded, and therefore it

---

[11] I'm not knocking these for what they are. I love case studies as I love stories, and I cherish hearing them. For the record, my kids will attest to the fact that I also love donkeys.

must clearly be due to all we observe or choose to observe within that organisation. There is a clear risk of survivorship bias in the interpretation of case studies. There is a wealth of studies you can delve into in this area should you wish to, including the work of Shermer (2014)[12] who explored how survivor bias changed people's perceptions of reality and how they perceived people and organisations to be successful or unsuccessful.

It is incredibly interesting to hear stories from other organisations of how they perceive they achieved change. I'm not suggesting we all start analysing data, reading research journals and ignore our HR networks doing interesting work and experiencing new things. We should continue to connect and to learn from each other's experience, but I would suggest we consider the following as we sit down to hear another case study:

- *Stay curious* – it can be very tempting to become overly focused on the process or the tool that another company used to create results, and assuming that this will solve your biggest HR issues. Remember to stay curious and ask, 'What else?' was shifting and changing when the impact was seen, what other variables were at play?

- *Be careful of seeking evidence to corroborate your existing arguments* – the real challenge here is how you see the similarities and tend not to see the dissimilarities, and it is within the dissimilarities that so much interesting information will sit.

---

[12] Shermer, M. (2014). 'How the survivor bias distorts reality'. *Scientific American*, Vol. 8, p. 19.

- *Don't be too tempted by the quick fix* – human nature and the complexities of leadership often cause us to pick the solutions that are not the best, but the easiest to implement.

Embracing innovation as a core HR skill and practice

Before we can understand how we can help our organisation and its people to be 'more innovative', we need to understand the meaning of innovation. What is innovation? For many of us, innovation means the introduction of new technology and inventions – such as the internet, apps and artificial intelligence. It is true that innovation led to the development of these tools and products, but innovation goes far beyond this. Innovation is often a collaborative, and potentially a community, activity. Thomas Edison, famous for inventing the lightbulb, didn't do this alone in a dark room until it finally worked. Edison patented 1,093 inventions before achieving his finest accolade, and he achieved all of this working alongside a dedicated team. Edison was certainly a genius, but it is his team that assimilated all his ideas, painstakingly tested them and finally achieved success.

In every organisation it is beneficial to reflect on whether people, processes and leadership are acting more as innovation enablers, or whether they are in fact acting as bottlenecks to potential new ideas or novel ways of working. Again, this does not mean copying what 'innovative companies' like Netflix are doing. Innovation and the creation of new products, services, tools and so on will look different from one organisation to another. So, how can we achieve innovation within our HR teams? We're often so steeped in the detail of operational HR activities that we have insufficient time to contemplate where we would like to innovate, let alone actually innovating. IBM completed a survey of global HR Leaders in 2010.[13] The results showed an agreement among HR Leaders that driving creativity and innovation is their number one business challenge, yet only 50% of these HR executives indicated that they are doing anything about it. This data is now eight years old, but I suspect very little has changed. We can support greater innovation in our practice through evidence-based practice and the avoidance of the hugely tempting affliction, case-study-itis. Other steps we might take to support innovation as an HR team are as follows:

1. *Start talking about innovation with your business leaders and all employees*

   o The ability to help create, maintain and build an organisational culture that fosters innovation is a critical role for HR. Making 'innovation' a core value and talking about how important it is won't create cultural change.

2. *Explore how your processes do or do not facilitate innovation*

   o Cultural change requires us to learn and develop the infrastructure for innovation, including the processes, collaborative technologies, flexibility of form and structure so that people can be free to think and to create new ideas.

3. *'What measures gets done', so how does your performance monitoring support innovation?*

   o Many organisations and many HR teams have an obsession with monitoring business results through

---

[13] www.ibm.com/services/insights/c-suite-study

monthly or quarterly performance reviews, with little emphasis on the longer-term plan. This monitoring activity can stifle innovation, through having a limited focus on longer-term planning.

4. *Celebrate innovative behaviours – hire, recognise and promote people who are innovative*

   ○ Is your potential new hire curious in their approach? Do they show an appetite to think differently and to test a range of options before coming to a conclusion? Are they open to new ideas, and to how these could be achieved?

   ○ Let people know that you value and measure success against core values such as innovation and ensure that you recognise and reward people who seek to innovate. I am always amazed when I see organisations celebrating an employee who has reached a certain period of time with the organisation, yet they don't reward employees for bringing in new ideas and practices.

5. *Develop the strategy and skills to support innovation in your people*

   ○ Innovation is often prized as the holy grail with little more than a strapline to make it happen. The first step to creating the change is to form a compelling vision for change, and to form a strategy alongside this that outlines why, how and with what you will create the shift toward innovation.

6. *Inspire your leaders and managers to be as enthusiastic about innovation as you are*

   ○ Encourage your line managers to be curious and supportive of innovative behaviours. This requires a collaborative and supportive team culture where people are encouraged to seek support to test their ideas, and where there is a culture that expects people to spend a proportion of their time testing and challenging their own, and others', ideas.

As HR professionals, helping your organisation to achieve greater innovation, to create a culture to support innovative thinking and to hire, train and reward is no mean feat. It can seem daunting to know where to begin. However, the most important first step is exploring the research further to understand what innovation could look like and the benefits it could bring to your organisation. It's a great starting point for evidence-based practice, and to see how far you can travel.

Summary

This chapter has explored how we might best approach developing new ways of working or new possibilities in Human Resources. We're seeking evidence to understand the impact a given intervention or activity may have. We will have isolated the impact or shift we want to create and through which intervention, and having tested that, we may have found this makes little to no difference. For example, we might test if enhanced pension schemes have any impact on employee engagement and on employee retention. The response may be 'no'. I wanted to leave this chapter with the, hopefully obvious, warning that there doesn't always need to be an evidence-base for 'doing the right thing'. Even if a course of action serves no meaningful purpose whatsoever for increasing performance or for increasing productivity, we might still invest in this course of action because it follows a moral imperative. Because we believe in 'people not paperclips'. The benefit of applying a spot of creativity to the issue and applying evidence-based practices means we know what the course of action will and won't achieve. This is supporting informed decision-making – it is as important to know what it won't achieve as what it will. In the next chapter we will shift our attention to the topic of 'change' and whether this can be managed or influenced at all. In short, if we have assessed the evidence-base, and we know we want to create organisational change, can we hope to orchestrate this in any meaningful way?

Toolkit B: Pause and reflect – what's possible, and what do I need to know to test this?

This toolkit for considering how you innovate and employ evidence-based practice in your own HR function or in your own HR or OD practice is clearly not exhaustive. I'm very aware that we all need to start somewhere and in forming the questions below, I've considered what would have been and continues to be useful to me when I consider 'what's possible, and what do I need to know to test this?'

1. *Isolate the area you want or need to focus on* – for example, you want to explore how to support the performance and career development of your people. You need to focus, even if that area itself feels really broad.

2. *Ask the simple question, 'What's possible here?'* – you could do this yourself, or as a team exercise, but seek as many views as possible before you move onto the next stage. I would strongly recommend that you take a free-writing approach. Just write down everything that comes into your mind and don't be restricted by your own experience of what has or hasn't worked in the past, or perhaps even by what others might think of your ideas. Collate the themes from this exercise, which will inform

---

next steps, and hopefully have also injected some energy and enthusiasm in you for the topic.

3. *Refine the area you are looking at even further, with the intention of developing a focused question or hypothesis for further research* – for example, are you still looking at the performance and career development of your people, or have you started to hone in on a specific area within this, for example building a feedback culture that will have multiple benefits beyond performance development? There may be multiple points of focus, but we're refining these into areas you can apply to a literature review or further exploration of the topic.

4. *Delve into the research* – you can put a time limit on it if you like, for example, I will explore the journals via the CIPD or another professional body for two hours on this topic, recording themes and findings as I go. I'm not trying to turn you into a researcher but flexing your analytical and research muscles will never go to waste as an HR practitioner. Imagine all the ER cases you can apply these to, or that in the future hopefully you won't need to.

5. *Consider what's possible, and what's new and novel out there* – has this been found to work in practice? You're now drawing together the various pieces to form recommendations for the next steps. You've explored what's possible and no doubt what is new or novel out there, you've honed down to a few fantastic possibilities, and you've sought to find some evidence for the impact these interventions have created.

6. *A problem shared is a problem reduced* – if there is no easily obtainable evidence-base, reach out to your

networks for support. Have they grappled with this area? Have they reached out to any interesting, expert parties for support? Building an evidence-base and sparking innovation isn't a solitary activity – remember Edison and his/his team's lightbulb and share your questions and challenges with others.

7. *Don't tie yourself up in knots – if the evidence isn't there for a solution, be part of testing that solution.* Sometimes the evidence-base hasn't been formed yet. That's ok. We regularly pilot activities to see their impact, and so it's unrealistic to suppose that we need a fully formed evidence-base before commencing anything in HR. By all means pilot a new approach or a new tool. The difference between a true pilot and just jumping on the fad-wagon is that pilots set out with evaluation criteria and seek feedback on these. They build the evidence-base, rather than bypass it.

These tips are intended to support each of us in taking a step toward evidence-based practice, or perhaps to support teams within your own organisation that are inspired to do the same.

Chapter 3

Can we really 'manage' cultural change?

Introduction

This book aims to support HR professionals to reimagine our organisations as more 'human', 'person-centred' environments and to seek strategies to make this happen. So, if we have a broad understanding of what motivates and engages people, and we know the importance of developing an evidence-base to support our innovations and intervention, are we all set? Sadly not. The change we create may still fall short of being a runaway success, or of actually creating any sustainable shift in how our organisation operates. We can commit to new approaches, we can communicate this to our people, and we can write a few papers and policies on the topic. It might have a project plan, perhaps even a stakeholder engagement map, and some risks and issues identified. We've probably got change agents and no doubt some 'Champions' lined up. We're busy managing change whilst change is just an ever constant happening 'out there'. As they say, life is what happens when you're busy making other plans. Take the example of how we support and develop our people. The old annual performance appraisal systems, most would agree, should give way to more fluid and continuous feedback. So we introduce a more fluid approach and tell everyone we want to 'trust' them and stop the tick-boxing approach. But still this doesn't result in our people reporting high engagement with our performance and career development processes. Are our people just extraordinarily high-maintenance, or have we missed a trick? It all made sense on the project plan, but the change hasn't had the impact we hoped for. Perhaps we can't 'manage' change after all.

This chapter will explore the notion of 'change management' in a people context. We will explore how the term Change Manager might make sense in how we implement new IT systems, but becomes far trickier as we try to effect how those same systems are adopted by real people, or seek to embed behavioural and cultural change. We'll explore how so much of what we call 'change management' is about project management, and the realms of cultural change are far harder to 'manage' in any way. This will lead onto a deeper exploration of 'culture', what it entails and how your own organisational culture, or that of your clients, may be observed or understood better. It may feel quite a swerve of a topic after delving into evidence-based practice in our previous chapter, but we'll make our way through the topic of storytelling to how you can harness stories to engage people and to connect your team and yourself to the people you support. Storytelling has always been part of human existence, long before language gave us the ability to articulate stories in words. The toolkit in this chapter will support you in thinking about the change you are seeking to create within your culture and discovering more about your starting point through exploring the different facets of your culture. You can approach the toolkit through the lens of your team culture or through your organisational culture; whatever is most impactful at this time for you.

Why change at all?

We often put forward project plans for 'change programmes' without providing a clear articulation for why we're proposing to change anything at all or, perhaps, why now? There is an opportunity to reflect on these areas before any action takes place, and to involve a wide set of stakeholders in considering why you would expend the energy and investment in such a process. Even when the reasons behind the change appear to be bleedingly obvious, I have witnessed great value in holding such dialogue. Considering 'Why change?' and 'Why now?' really tests the sponsors and people leading the process to consider the evidence-base again, and to clearly articulate a rationale that will form part of the key stakeholder messaging throughout any change process. Leap over this stage of the change process, and I suspect you'll spend twice the time and efforts later in the process retro-fitting key communications and managing the fall-out from unclear messaging.

Introducing the paradoxical nature of change

There is a story I once read, describing the work of Professor James Barker of Marquette University. Barker found that even the best intended of management initiatives can evolve in weird and wonderful ways. Studying one organisation's transformation from a traditional hierarchy to self-managing teams, Barker was surprised to find that the change produced even tighter control than what existed under the old-fashioned hierarchy. They set out to achieve one thing, and the outcome was far removed from that intended. Ronald, one of the technical employees Barker interviewed for the study, told him that he felt more closely watched under the new, apparently 'egalitarian system'. Whilst his former boss might have overlooked him coming in a little late occasionally, for example, his team had a 'no tolerance' policy on tardiness. They monitored members' behaviours closely and imposed sanctions for non-compliance. I've worked in teams before where the leadership were perfectly supportive of flexible working and home working too, but the team members frowned upon people not being seen to 'pull their weight'. Again, this research poses the question, can we really manage change?

Organisations hire 'Change Managers', consultants and so-called experts to manage change. I have never talked about holding any skill in 'managing change' because I believe it's the stuff of make-believe; about as useful as me charging a day rate to show up with fairy dust. Project and programme managers can certainly lead changes to how processes and people are managed. They can lead behavioural change through introducing new processes and ways of working to comply with. When it comes to cultural change, the change that many organisations state they are working on, we seldom focus on more than one part of the organisation system. We say we are seeking cultural change through developing our leaders, or through introducing new 'values'. It's seen as academic or time-wasting to spend too long understanding the concept of 'culture' or what might underpin this, so that we might take a more informed approach or at least be more realistic about what we can and can't achieve via a project plan.

I worked in a team of Occupational Psychologists for the Ministry of Defence, and more specifically the Royal Air Force, one of the most wonderful cultures I have ever worked in. The intellectual capital sitting within that organisation is mind-blowing and hugely inspiring to me. We were fortunate to work on some high-profile cultural change 'programmes' of work that required an in-depth understanding of the sub-cultures within parts of the organisation. One of our Senior Psychologists at the time mapped out what makes a 'culture'; the stories told within the organisation, the artefacts that you see within the organisation (what is on the wall, what is seen around the office), the language people do and don't use, the leadership structures and how these play out in practice, and so on. The reason we can't 'manage' cultural change is because we so rarely delve into these important aspects of organisational culture. We also rarely appreciate that 'culture' isn't all-encompassing. There are sub-cultures within organisations, and it is these sub-cultures that people attach themselves to and that they refer to when reporting on their engagement at work. It's hugely complex, and if we fail to appreciate this, and to realise 'culture change' is best approached from the realm of behavioural science and systemic change than from a project spreadsheet, we set ourselves up to never quite reach our desired outcomes.

What is the benefit of understanding the nuances of a culture through exploring with curiosity the stories, language and artefacts in an organisation? The benefit is that we approach 'change management' in a more human way. It stops us from over-simplifying change as who is 'positive' and who 'resists' change. It also gives us the opportunity to reframe the stories people are telling, to understand and respond to the importance they may place on the symbols and celebrations they hold onto within their culture, and to tailor change approaches accordingly. An example may be the reaction leadership in an organisation experience when they change an approach brought in by the founder of the company. Employees express anger and this is perceived to be people not recognising the need for change and progress. 'They're dinosaurs', 'they don't understand' and so on. If we delved into the stories people tell, it may be that this approach was part of the organisation's heritage, it was part of the pride people placed in their work and how they talked about it to others. Understanding culture in greater depth, and seeking to build a 'softer' evidence-base beyond employee surveys allows us to get under the skin of what resistance really is. I'm sure it doesn't feel like there's a great deal of time for qualitative research or 'asking your people about the culture' in greater depth, but so many interventions that steam on without this understanding fail.

The power of stories in exploring and embedding cultural change

Under suits and uniforms are stories. I can't remember where I read that line, so credit to whoever first said it. It is so true though. I really want to spend more time exploring storytelling with you. This topic has been covered through a marketing lens, through sociology and psychology, and I'll also bring in some OD thinking at points. The reality is that our lives and our working lives are socially fabricated, beautiful messes, all built upon shedloads of stories. It is these colourful experiences that shape people into who they are, and into the unique individuals that collectively contribute to what makes an organisation unique. We would hope that all key organisational decisions should be based on objectivity and rational analysis of the facts, but once we've decided on a course of action or are still in the information-gathering phase, we need to focus on how to create behavioural change, and the next step that is true attitude change (the gold at the end of the rainbow for OD consultants). It is here that storytelling can be a powerful tool to create and support cultural change.

Storytelling evokes a neurological response in all of us; our brains are wired to hear and respond to stories. Our brain produces the stress hormone cortisol during the tense moment in a story, which allows us to focus, whilst the emotional or positive aspects of a story release oxytocin, the feel-good brain chemical that promotes empathy and human connection. We can use these in our communications regarding change, but we can also listen and hear the stories others tell to understand what is important to them and the 'truth' or perspectives they hold. This may all be starting to feel very theoretical, perhaps all a little pointless? I share this thinking because I believe it has the power to create a mindset shift in how HR operate. I want us to step back and stop doing 'stuff'. If nothing else, I want to inspire us as a profession to take off our practitioner hats and to work from a place of curiosity to get under the skin of what is going on within our organisations.

I will give you an example of how I have seen storytelling unleash challenges within cultures, and to facilitate behavioural change at the individual level. The Royal Air Force has long had a strong focus on diversity and inclusion, and during my time there they were working with a forum theatre company that brought forum theatre to explore and to tackle unconscious bias. At the time, over ten years ago, this was quite a pioneering concept. We watched a play where a group of people were going camping. One of the people camping was a blind man. Another character in the play asked them about themselves, and expressed surprise when they talked about their family, their kids and their social life and interests. The character was taken aback as they had an unconscious story or picture in their head of someone blind living alone with their guide-dog and having limited social interests due to their disability. The stories and beliefs they had coloured their reactions to this person – they were perfectly pleasant in the story, but they didn't engage with the blind person as an equal, and acted like they needed to mollycoddle or 'look after' this person. I can still remember a member of our audience sharing in the Q&A afterwards that this point of the story had been a borderline epiphany for them. It had raised their awareness of their own personal unconscious biases and had given them the opportunity to rethink and retell the stories of people with disability that they held. We can use stories to explore and to tackle issues, and to understand the stories employees hold. We can't scale up change to a project plan and forget that what we're really dealing with is a collection of minds. We don't 'manage' cultural change; we explore, understand and shift mindsets and ways of working.

Telling stories in HR to engage and inspire people

We've explored that it's difficult to 'manage' change. We've explored how culture is made up of a complex myriad of factors, including stories. Given the importance of storytelling to human nature and human history, it seems useful to touch on how we can leverage the use of stories to support our own communication within HR. Telling authentic and personal stories about your organisation is one of the most powerful tools you as a leader can use to drive and sustain employee engagement. David Macleod and Nita Clarke produced a paper in 2009 as part of an employee engagement taskforce for the former UK coalition government. The research intended to explore factors that drive employee engagement and productivity. They found that one of the primary drivers of employee engagement is exposure to leaders who can articulate a clear narrative (or story) about their organisation. These leaders are always talking about where their organisation has come from, where it is now, and most importantly where it is going in the future. We need to encourage our leaders to do this, but we also need to start with ourselves in HR.

So, how can you tell a powerful story about the change you are seeking to create in HR? Stories that people can personally connect to are the most powerful. And the best way to find these stories is through understanding what your people perceive to be important, what excites or interests them, and using this as the hook for your story.

Stories may fall into one of three categories:

• First, there are *stories from the past* – these illustrate the history and background or the inherent shared purpose and values of your organisation: this might be how the organisation has survived through adversity to growing and succeeding, or it could be how you personally as a leader have achieved this. The reason people ask about each other's backgrounds is to understand these stories – they are seeking to understand and to connect at a deeper level. The question, 'Where do you work?' is an example of people seeking information to build a story for themselves about you. Fast-track this by telling them your own authentic story, or the story of your function or organisation.

- *Stories from the present* – these might be recognition of current successes or lessons learned. These celebrate the hard work, ingenuity and successes of team members in meeting organisational challenges, developing quality products or services and championing the needs of customers. These stories are the ones we often hear in employee recognition schemes, and are an important part of building an ongoing feedback culture in organisations.

- *Stories about the future* – this is your opportunity to paint a picture about your vision and the roadmap for how you can achieve this for, and with, others. This is a hugely important story to tell, and one that requires a truly honest, authentic approach. It is possible to draw on the stories of the past and present to form a rationale for why the future is needed, but it requires a story of its own. I'm a visual person and I'm particularly energised by leaders painting a picture in my mind of the future they wish to create. Holding an image in my mind of that future supports me in managing challenges in the present and allows me to start to reframe any inconsistencies in how I envisaged that future looking. There may be so much ambiguity in the future that it feels like our story would be unclear, that picture would be a little hazy, and that's ok. Ask people to tell a story for how they would like the future to look and why. It is through these shared stories that compelling visions and strategies can be built. Beyond structured strategy development timelines and conference room flipchart paper, so many future visions and plans are actually built on the back of powerful storytelling.

This isn't a book about how to structure and tell an incredible story. However, these are a few, potentially useful, tips that I've observed from watching some brilliant storytellers in action:

1. *If you don't look excited, don't expect your audience to be –* storytelling is a performance and you need energy and enthusiasm to tell a good story. I can remember watching a conference presenter talk about their research, which they described as 'exciting'. I've never seen anyone look as bored as they said it. Your body language needs to mirror your story – if you look like you're close to horizontal and snoring, you can guarantee a few of your audience actually will be. In all honesty, some of the best stories you'll hear won't even be the most interesting nor the wildest. This is where observational comedy gets its fans from; sometimes the most mundane is the most comical or entertaining when you can share this to connect with your audience.

2. *People can hear a smile, or indeed a tear –* well they can't really, but you can tell if a person is smiling as they tell a story, even via the phone due to small changes in the tone of their voice. A smile isn't always appropriate. I can still remember a Director at a charity I worked for crying during a presentation. It wasn't hugely unusual; death and suffering of small children often did, and should, arouse high emotion amongst colleagues who believe in the cause to alleviate this suffering. The tears demonstrated that they weren't just telling a story of something 'happening over there' – this is and was real life and we were all part of the story.

3. *Keep it snappy* – as I not-so-hilariously say to my small children, 'Make me a crocodile sandwich. And make it snappy.' Long stories risk confusing the audience and testing the emotional connection of even the most interested of audiences. This doesn't mean that your stories need to turn into a series of snappy one-liners, but you do need to test yourself on how much content you really need and want to get your key points across.

4. *Paint a picture* – as I said earlier, really paint a picture for your audience with your stories. Whilst this doesn't require an all-day storytelling session (see above), it does require some context-setting, some facts and observations, so that the audience can picture this in their minds.

Toolkit C: Reflecting on your culture

This toolkit will be an opportunity for you to consider 'where you are now' in your team or organisation from a cultural standpoint. You will obviously need to define where you're heading, and why, but getting under the skin of your starting point is so important. Think of it as the psychotherapy of cultural change – understanding what is going on within the psyche of your organisation, in order to influence and shape your future. I did warn you that I love psychology.

Exploring culture through what you see, hear and experience within your culture

I would like you to spend time exploring, noting down and asking others about some of the key components of an organisational culture listed below. Note, these are not intended to be exhaustive.

1. *What does your organisation tell the world about who and what it is there to serve?*

   What is your organisation's vision, mission and strategy? How is this articulated, and are your people aware of what each element means in practice? Together these elements contribute to a common purpose for your people and will support how they view themselves adding to your organisational vision and potentially to society, and to how they interact with each other. The interesting bit here is not even if you do have a vision statement, the interesting bit is whether there is a gap between that vision statement and the lived experience of your employees. Do you say one thing, but do another? Is there a lack of clarity regarding what you're seeking to achieve, which might leave your people in a state of confusion, or even pointing their efforts in the wrong direction? You can discover all this through looking at company communications and what you observe in those around you, or read and hear about via employee feedback.

2. *Does your organisation live its values?*

   Are these values lived throughout your people's everyday actions? What is celebrated and talked about in your organisation? A company's values are the core of its culture. Whilst a vision articulates a company's purpose, values offer a set of guidelines on the behaviours and mindsets needed to achieve that vision. You can discover more about how closely your organisation or your people are putting these values into action through observing your people in action, and through delving into a range of data including employee feedback, leadership communications and exit interview feedback.

Again, how far the values are put into action through behaviours, and who does or does not live the values, is far more interesting than whether the actual words are on placards anywhere. Though where the words are placed around the organisation is of relevance here too.

3. *What language is used within the organisation – how do people speak with each other and of each other?*
   The language used within an organisation, perhaps the use of acronyms, banter or 'in-jokes', will all tell you about an organisation and its culture. Do people use language to bring others into discussion or to demarcate who is part or not part of the 'in-group'? Language and how we talk to each other can be a powerful mechanism for excluding people, and it is therefore an important consideration when exploring organisational culture. Do we tell people that we are an 'innovative culture where people are valued and respected' and then in practice people join, are barely spoken to and are only invited out for an evening if they are seen to fit in? You get my point.

4. *Heritage, symbols and artefacts.*
   The museum of your organisation, no less. Even start-ups have stories to tell about their histories, and the symbols of what is important to them and their success. I worked in one start-up which was set up by a group of highly talented ex-colleagues from an IT consultancy background. Symbols of the organisation included an open invitation to anyone in the office to join in office drinks, the expectation that people would socialise widely and enjoy each other's company and the addition of family days on an annual basis. What

did this tell me about the organisation? It told me that this was an organisation that wanted to create a family feel where people were valued. All organisations have a unique context. The ability to uncover, to explore and to communicate that history in a compelling way is part of how we create our cultures, and part of how we maintain the status quo. If you're seeking cultural change, you need to uncover the heritage, the symbols and the artefacts within your own organisation that contribute to that organisational narrative.

In the Royal Air Force, there were actual museums to celebrate its strong heritage, in other organisations there are trophies in the foyer or pictures of the founder on the wall. We celebrate 50th anniversaries of when organisations were founded – this stuff is important to us, and I hope it's interesting reminding yourself of what is celebrated in your organisation, what pictures make the foyer and which are relegated to the toilet and so on?

5. *Observing ways of working in your organisation.*
    and their expectation Your values talk about collaboration, you've just implemented agile working, yet in practice people report working in silos and having limited accountability over how they achieve their work. You're looking for the grey areas here – how is the work really achieved? Do people work flexibly or is that really 'lip service' from your HR policy, and no one can actually make this work in practice? Do you run well-being sessions and have an in-house masseur and counselling service, but actually it's underused and your

absence rates due to workplace stress are growing each month?

6. *The stories you hear and tell within your culture.*
   I've saved this magic for last, having spent quite a bit of this chapter selling the benefit of looking at this exact topic.

I'm hoping you've got enough tips to dive in. There are other factors that influence culture. But these six components can provide a firm foundation for shaping a new organisation's culture. And identifying and understanding them more fully in an existing organisation can be the first step to revitalising or reshaping culture in a company looking for change.

You're exploring all of this to get under the skin of your culture. You are building a picture of what we might term your 'as is' picture. This provides you with a strong baseline so that you can see how far you need to travel to achieve whatever your 'to be' picture might be.

SECTION TWO

CREATING A PEOPLE-FOCUSED CULTURE

Chapter 4

Can Organisation Development put the human back into Human Resources?

Introduction

This is the section when we really start looking into the worlds of Organisation Development and occupational psychology to understand how we can create person-focused cultures that care. This chapter will ask what Organisation Development as a skill set and a broader profession can bring to the discussion. This is a huge topic to cover in a single chapter, and I won't even set myself the high bar of 'doing it justice'. I will instead refer you at key points to incredible further reading in the area from some true Organisation Development gurus (who, I have no doubt, despise the word 'guru').

I will deep-dive into the topic of 'curiosity' as a skill set that I think could add great value in any team, and which I would suggest sets good OD practitioners apart from great OD practitioners in our profession. Working without judgement, with positive intent and with true curiosity are the true strengths or qualities of great OD practitioners, and certainly embody the fabulous practitioners I will quote in this book. I'll provide you with some tips and techniques for applying these skills in your own HR practice, and the toolkit at the end of the chapter will explore how you can draw on OD practice within your own HR team to create greater impact.

Applying OD to the field of HR

What is 'Organisation Development'? OD is a profession based on humanistic principles, which strives to develop our understanding of human dynamics at work and how we can apply this knowledge to create 'healthy' organisations. Whilst we often draw on OD interventions within teams or perhaps with a group of leaders, the intent is always to impact on the organisation as a system. OD practitioners seek to diagnose issues within organisations, involving leaders and employees in responding to people challenges, and supporting the organisation to be fit for purpose for the future. Part of the core skill set of an OD practitioner is therefore to hold a mirror up to the organisation and to challenge unhealthy aspects of the system. I've often been told that I'm 'too nice to work in HR' (I hope this isn't too unbelievable for those who have actually worked with me) and a recent social media post on this topic really resonated with me. The post noted that there is a difference between being 'nice' and being 'kind' and that the latter requires a certain candour, or honesty, that can mean being uncomfortable to support the awareness or learning of others. This, for me, is OD in practice. This is the humanistic element in play. With positive intent and with the humility that we don't need or want to 'be right', we hold a mirror up to support and challenge another person's thinking, as we hope they would for us. The opportunities to apply the principles, knowledge and skills from OD within the HR profession are huge, and I would argue this is still relatively untapped within many organisations.

There has been much debate about whether OD is a field of practice and a profession in its own right. There has long been a blurred line between OD and HR. This blurred line has threatened to place Organisation Development in the same camp as 'employee engagement'; little more than a transient job title that gets changed quicker than the hemlines at London

Fashion Week. In fact, in many organisations, OD is singled out as a skill set or sub-team within the Human Resource function. OD is also mapped as one of the core skills areas of an HR Leader in the Chartered Institute of Personnel & Development's HR Professions Career Map. I'm quite clear where I sit on this one, and it isn't on a fence. OD is a profession in its own right, and not a tool or skill set that can be absorbed into another profession, or a new term for a learning function, dependent on what the person with the title 'OD Consultant' has in their skill set. I make this point as a self-confessed career hybrid. I identify as an Occupational Psychologist over being an OD practitioner, and have no great yearning to be seen as an HR expert at all. In truth, I'd like to be known as someone who is curious about the application of behavioural science to how we work, but that doesn't make for a snappy title on social media. I used to think, 'Who cares where OD sits anyway?' But on reflection, how OD relates to the Human Resources function really does matter. For if we package OD up as an HR skill, it risks losing some of its independence, and therein loses some of its potential to make a difference. OD really needs to sit across the business, taking a helicopter view of the organisation in order to have optimal impact. We need to be mindful about not losing the importance of OD as a profession that comes with deep expertise in systems theory, and a multitude of tools and models that can bring impact to the world of work. I share this here because in gaining an awareness of OD theories and knowledge, we should also gain an awareness of the limitations of our own practice and when we would benefit from developing our knowledge or seeking the technical expertise of someone more learned in the field. I hope this chapter will help you to achieve just that.

Many OD professionals within HR departments focus on employee experience or employee engagement, whilst others are responsible for developing the capability of leaders and the broader employee group. Whilst this is all incredibly important work, it is focusing on a single component of the organisational system, and not looking systemically across the organisation to achieve impact. Whilst learning and development focuses on how individuals and teams can develop and grow their capability; on human potential, OD focuses on human dynamics. The tools and knowledge available to us from the field of OD help us to understand how people and organisations work, and to create the right environment across the organisational system for this to occur. As long as we support all practitioners to have a good understanding of how to use OD principles, tools, techniques, concepts and processes, then wherever it sits, it will make a difference, and that's all that really matters. Which leads me onto how we can apply OD thinking within the field of HR. OD offers great potential for bringing greater humanity into Human Resources and the wider world of work. Instead of being based on processes and practices, and HR manuals and policies, it focuses on the more strategic side of people management and development, and on how we can ensure we are addressing cultural challenges and opportunities to build work environments where people can flourish. It promises to take HR from mitigating risks and enforcing policies to embedding the organisation's values through its people's behaviours and ways of working. OD brings core principles of trust in people, and a belief in the importance of employee empowerment, and places skills such as curiosity and self-awareness centre stage. OD is less about a toolkit that HR people can draw on, than a way of being we can adopt and practice through our work.

Mee-Yan Cheung-Judge, one of the Founders of the NTL Institute in the UK, describes OD practitioners as using their sense of 'self as an instrument'[14] in their work. They themselves are the tool that creates the difference in their work, and this creates high responsibility on the OD practitioner to operate in a way that is true to the principles of OD; in a human-centred, transparent, fair and open way. This way of being is central to holding positive power dynamics within the organisation, to creating client-helping relationships that empower rather than frustrate, and to being what is often termed a 'humble enquirer' in OD-speak. In this chapter, I will share more about each of these aspects of OD. Each of these skills or tools offer us the opportunity to put greater humanity and care into our work as HR professionals through considering the impact of our behaviours and interventions on people and their individual needs.

Learning from the consultancy phases of Organisation Development

There are some key phases of an Organisation Development consultancy cycle that will be important and useful to reflect on as HR professionals. Even when operating as an internal business partner, we are offering our internal consultancy skills to support the business. These OD 'phases' will be viewed and conceptualised differently dependent on the OD consultancy or consultant you speak with. As a general rule you would expect to find the following high-level activities occurring in an OD 'project'. You might revisit certain stages repeatedly through the process, and start at various points of entry, but the key

---

[14] Cheung-Judge, M. (2001). 'Use of self as an instrument: A cornerstone for the future of OD'. *OD Practitioner*, Vol. 33, p. 3.

components required to facilitate a process, rather than to offer an intervention, are as follows:

- Entry and contracting

- Evidence and information gathering

- Diagnosis and prioritisation

- Implementation

- Feedback and evaluation

- Ending the relationship, or re-contracting.

I will explore these in a little more depth, so that you can consider how far you apply the given skills and activities in your organisational context. Each time a stakeholder comes to you with a problem, you should be able to apply the thinking from these OD phases to support them in finding a solution and putting this in place. For example, a stakeholder tells you, 'My department are disengaged and productivity has fallen. I think it's due to the top team, but I don't know what to do.' Instead of leaping into advice mode, you consider the support you could offer, enter into dialogue with them on the issue, and enter into the OD phases with the intention of supporting *their* solution, rather than giving them *your* solution to implement.

1. *Entry and contracting*

    We all 'contract' or set expectations with others – this is part of everyday human dynamics. We need to understand what is expected of us, what we can expect of others in any given human exchange, and how we might resolve conflict should it arise. Whilst formal contracts are typically drawn up in commercial consultancy arrangements, 'contracting' in its broadest sense is valuable in all your interactions with your client or customer. In this phase, you will explore the problem your client is experiencing, you will explore their motivations and what is important to them, and you will define who the client is. The latter might sound obvious, but often the person who first approaches us to share the problem is not our key stakeholder, and we need to determine who this person is.

Listening skills are imperative to successful contracting, as is a strong sense of self-awareness from you with regard to your own capabilities and how you can best support your client. During the contracting phase, you will be seeking to understand the part you can play in supporting the client, and this requires openness and honesty regarding your own limitations and where you can best add value. The reason the contracting phase is so often re-visited throughout the consulting cycle is that what is needed may change, you or your client might feel that some or all of your expectations aren't being met as agreed at the outset, and you may wish to give each other feedback. Contracting is vital to supporting a continual feedback loop, and contracting skills should be a hugely valuable part of any HR Leader's skill set.

2. *Evidence and information gathering*
   We have explored the importance of evidence-based practice, so I won't labour the point again here. A core component of practising OD is the collation of information or data that will test and support the interventions that follow. In fact, one of the key reasons for collating data at all is to test if any intervention at all is needed. This requires skills in data collection, including, potentially, survey administration and analysis, interview skills, action learning or focus group facilitation and a whole host of other potential OD tools and techniques. When one of your key stakeholders comes to you with an issue, you might say, 'I'll look into this for you'. Even if you don't kick-start survey and interview research

as a result, it's important to know what's available and to make an informed decision on just how much information gathering is required to inform your next steps.

When you are supporting a major change, for example leading an organisation design project to ensure your organisation is fit for purpose for the future, you will need to do extensive information gathering to support your perceptions of the current state and your judgement of what the future state should look like. There won't necessarily be the skills and capabilities within your own team to achieve this. Having a high-level understanding of what good looks like, and the wealth of tools out there to support information gathering, will stand you in good stead as you procure external consultancy support for this. There are many OD workshops that focus on the evidence and information-gathering phase, and I would strongly recommend investing time in attending one if you don't already hold strong skills in this area.

3. *Diagnosis and prioritisation*

Following information gathering is a key phase of synthesis and analysis of that information. You will find that many OD practitioners talk about a 'diagnostic' phase or a phase when they consider what the information is telling them, and what this means for next steps in resolving the issue posed by their stakeholder. There may be a great wealth of potential actions that could be taken, and it is here that these need to be considered and prioritised. One of the key pitfalls in any profession, and HR is no different, is that we are overly ambitious about what we can achieve. There is a saying that we overestimate what we can achieve in a year, and underestimate what we can achieve in ten years. If we're in the business of cultural and behavioural change, we are playing the long game, and need to be mindful of over-burdening ourselves with a myriad of activities in the misplaced belief that this will result in success.

4. *Implementation*

The favourite OD phase of those people who just want to 'get it done' is the implementation phase. This is where, as an HR professional, you might plan out a series of interventions with your client group that will take place over a reasonable timescale, and will define criteria for success. Considering the change you want to create at the forefront of this phase is very important. Evaluation can often be seen as something that is 'done' at the end of a project or programme of work, whilst it should always be considered upfront.

The implementation phase is about more than just getting stuff done. The process you follow will always be just as important, if not more so, than the outcome you achieve at the end. How you approach implementation, the dialogue you create as you put the interventions in place, will all send key messages to your people. Conducting this phase successfully requires deep expertise in process consultation or how processes operate in groups. You can build this expertise through further development in OD or through working with someone who holds this expertise already – the key thing to remember here is that you can undo all your great work from effective contracting and information gathering if you just land solutions on people at this stage. Ensuring the process reflects a person-centred, inclusive approach is imperative in a context where we are seeking to create person-centred cultures.

5. *Feedback and evaluation*

As discussed, seeking feedback and evaluating progress within your work can easily end up in the 'too hard box'. This need not be so. And it is never a waste of time if you seek to do it properly. The first step in seeking feedback and evaluating progress is to build a trusting relationship with your client. Being able to confidently and genuinely test how far a process has been of value to the organisation requires honesty and openness.

Imagine you are working with your client groups on a change project to embed new behaviours in your organisation. In this example, you may define the evaluation criteria through: a) understanding why the change is being introduced, and b) determining the key factors that test if a change has taken place. In considering b), it can be very difficult to select factors that are not moderated by a number of other variables throughout the change process. For example, you might use retention data as one source of evaluation criteria, yet this is also influenced by market conditions and other engagement factors.

6. *Ending the relationship, or re-contracting*
   Even as an internal consultant or practitioner, you need to develop your skills at ending a relationship. This is important to prevent dependency building on your skills, and to ensure you are building the skills within the system to take the change forward. In OD, we are always seeking to develop sustainable solutions and to support the skills of those people we work with. As an HR professional working with a client group, 'ending the relationship' may mean having a project closure meeting and defining what 'business as usual' responsibilities look like in the future. Or it might mean marking the end of the support from external consultants and transitioning responsibility to the internal HR team.

This is a brief introduction or refresher of the key phases of the OD consultancy cycle, and is intended to remind you of the importance of relationship-building and expectation setting throughout our work with our client groups. We will now go on to explore a key skill that will come in hugely useful as you navigate your way through the consultancy cycle; curiosity.

Curiosity as a key skill in OD, HR and for leadership in general

Curiosity – a state of active interest or genuinely wanting to know more about something – allows us to embrace unfamiliar circumstances, and to discover and learn more about the world around us. Curiosity is fundamental to how we learn and develop our thinking, and to how we broaden that thinking to operate in an inclusive manner. Research, including that led by Kang et al. (2009)[15] suggests that curiosity can trigger learning pathways in the brain, resulting in stronger recall of information. Curiosity was also found to facilitate learning behaviours like asking questions, exploration and experimentation, researching and seeking solutions, and to trial different ways of achieving an outcome. These experiments, and many others, have found that curiosity tends toward asking more insightful questions of those around us. The research by Kang found that a curious person demonstrated the ability to explore a topic with purpose and to maintain an open mind to alternative views. Curiosity was at one time considered to be a personality trait – something that is fixed. The literature now suggests that it is more fluid, and that we can develop and stretch our levels of curiosity. We are all curious about some things more than others, and we tend to become more curious about things as interest in them is ignited by a little knowledge.

---

[15] Kang M. J. et al. (2009). 'The wick in the candle of learning: epistemic curiosity activates reward circuitry and enhances memory'. *Psychological Science*, Vol. 20, pp. 963–973.

So how can you demonstrate curiosity, and continue to build your curiosity muscles as an HR practitioner?

1. *Always ask questions*
   What journalists call 'the five W's and the H' – who, what, when, where, why and how – are our tools of the curiosity trade. Curiosity is making the choice to look deeper into everyday things and to uncover something you weren't aware of before. Ask questions and listen as opposed to quickly searching for answers to a problem. Also acknowledge when you don't know the answer. This highlights to others that it's alright to be guided by curiosity.

2. *Explore unusual connections*
   Lucy Adams, ex-HR Director for the BBC and founder of Disruptive HR, has brought a great deal of learning from the world of marketing into HR via her books and workshops.[16] This is both hugely refreshing and hugely impactful for the profession. Stay curious and think what you can learn from others around you, however unusual, and apply it back into your own HR toolkit.

3. *Recognise how a lack of curiosity holds you back*
   Bureaucracy is probably the primary reason why HR departments find it so difficult to move from a transactional role to a more strategic, transformational one. Creating a culture of curiosity within your organisation, and in your own team, is one way of moving away from bureaucratic practices. Ask how can we do things differently around here? What do other organisations do, and why?

---

[16] Adams, L. (2017). *HR Disrupted: It's Time for Something Different.* Practical Inspiration Publishing: London.

4. *Suspend judgement*

The enemy of curiosity is pre-judging a situation or assuming you know the answer. Keep an open mind, as far as possible, and stay curious. For example, you can't possibly know how every client meeting will go with a tricky client, so don't walk in prepared for the person to be as tricky as ever, or readily label them as 'painful'. Stick with it, stay curious, and consider why you're observing what you are in that person. It's a complex world out there, you'll be relieved to not have to pretend to yourself you have the answers anymore.

Operating with humility – the concept of the 'humble enquirer'

We've explored what OD is and where it might sit, or tends to sit, within an organisation. And we've explored curiosity as a central tenet of OD practitioners, and arguably a central tenet of any person in the world of work. I would now like to introduce you to another model within OD that promises to have a sizeable impact on how we interact with our client groups, and on how we view our role as HR professionals within our organisations. This is the concept of 'humble enquiry', introduced by the 'father of OD', Ed Schein. Humble enquiry is a way of being, and it has the power to really bring the 'human' centre stage in Human Resources.[17]

So, why so 'humble'? Ed Schein describes humble enquiry as entering into, supporting, or working with others in full recognition of the fact that we don't have all the right answers up our sleeve. We don't need to move into 'expert' mode to have impact, and if we're confident in our own ability and practice,

---

[17] Schein, E. H. (2013). *Humble Inquiry: The Gentle Art of Asking Instead of Telling*. Berrett-Koehler Publishers: Oakland, CA.

we really shouldn't need to constantly wear the 'expert' hat. We're not going to change their world with a few PowerPoint slides or pre-prepared workshop outlines, and offering a listening ear and asking powerful questions to understand is more likely to create impact. Schein proposes that we should operate as curious and 'humble' practitioners, working with our client groups to discover what is occurring in their teams or organisations, and not to hurry to a solution for a pre-supposed issue. In reality, so many HR professionals and consultants alike already think they have the solution and they are overly keen to make recommendations, either to speed up the solution or born out of the belief that they are expected to have all the answers. In Schein's more eloquent words, humble enquiry is 'the skill and the art of drawing someone out, of asking questions to which you do not already know the answer, of building a relationship based on curiosity and interest in the other person'. The concept of humble enquiry reminds us that good questioning requires that we set aside our egos and stay curious. As noted, it can be particularly difficult for leaders to ask the questions they feel they should already know the answer to. Many leaders believe their role is to tell people what to do, and to be a humble enquirer therefore requires a certain comfort with showing vulnerability. Humble enquiry offers a way to achieve open and transparent communication between the hierarchies of an organisation, through leaders being encouraged to ask open questions of each other. It offers a mechanism for ensuring that all people are heard and listened to on the basis of their ideas and thoughts, rather than on the positional power that they hold. In this way, it offers a double whammy for bringing a people focus to the workplace.

'Helping behaviour' is another key concept from Ed Schein that can support us HR professionals to build stronger relationships, and to foster stronger collaboration between us and our colleagues. Surely 'helping' someone else is pretty straightforward, I hear you say. That's what we're here for as HR professionals. No. Much of what we describe as 'helping' behaviour in HR is actually giving others a solution, which keeps us firmly in the role of 'expert' and them in the more vulnerable role of needy recipient of our help. It remains a mind-boggling fact of human nature that our generous efforts to help others often leads to rejection, frustration, or even resentfulness from the other person. Schein offers an insight into why this happens – he suggests that every time we are in a position where someone may require our support, a 'helping event', it is 'unbalanced and ambiguous' in nature and therefore there is the risk that one or more participants could feel disempowered or embarrassed as a result of the exchange. Over-complicating a simple offer of help? Perhaps, but read on because this stuff really matters as an internal or external consultant. Schein advises that, 'Needing help often feels demeaning. It is a loss of independence to have someone else advise you.' If being asked to help provides us with a gain in status, then asking for help indicates an inability to help ourselves and is, of course, a loss of status. And this is one of the reasons I love OD – it illuminates areas that are sometimes taken for granted, and in doing so, it really allows us the opportunity to reassess our behaviour and the impact of our behaviour. We should apply this thinking to how we explore organisational issues with our client groups, and how we respond to these issues. Before offering help, we should explore if the other party are already in a position to find a solution, and we should also reflect if we are best placed to offer help.

Schein[18] suggests that we should choose the role that will best serve and support the relationship when we are tempted to give help.

---

[18] Schein, E. (2011). *Helping: How to Offer, Give, and Receive Help.* Berrett-Koehler Publishers: Oakland, CA.

At times, we may operate in an expert role offering guidance, at other times we may be listening and diagnosing a problem, and at others again we may be an enquiring consultant. The skill comes in knowing when and how to move between these different roles to best meet the needs of the client and the organisation, rather than to serve the needs of our own egos. In the spirit of reducing our ever-present egos (and we all have them, it's par for the course of being a human being), we must consider our intention before offering another person or party 'help'. And we should be clear on what is being asked and why. For example, a leader may be asking for help for one of their team, but the team member themselves doesn't believe they need it. Our goal therefore is to understand why the help is being asked for, and to determine what will best serve the needs of that person, or it is likely to land poorly.

Unlocking the power of human dynamics

Building your own awareness of team dynamics and that of your HR team, if you have one, has enormous potential for 'putting the human back into HR'. There is little more 'human' than how we interact with each other. We are social animals, and the workplace is one of the most important contexts in which social behaviour plays out. Team dynamics make or break team performance, and ultimately have a huge impact on organisational performance and potential. In essence, if we don't understand the processes and interactions that occur in groups, we reduce our capacity to impact on these. Whilst it's genuinely positive and important that many HR professionals are now business savvy and financially literate, if only as many had put their noses into a book on occupational psychology or human dynamics. Research on group processes and group dynamics is like HR power fuel. The knowledge allows us to work alongside the business to understand the root cause of issues, and to pinpoint interventions that will create change.

One of my favourite books on OD is called *A Field Guide for Organisation Development*, by Griffin et al. (2014).[19] One of the finest chapters is penned by Penny Lock, an OD expert and consultant, and is titled 'Could you come and do something with my team?' One sentence on team development that says it all. If I had a pound for every time a manager or leader has said those words to me, I'd be both a cliché and a few hundred pounds richer. As an internal consultant or HR Leader, team development or the oft dreaded 'away day' is usually scheduled because a new strategy is being developed, or perhaps a few people haven't been getting on. As an external consultant, in my experience, people get in touch for support because a team away day has been scheduled in the diary and the leader isn't sure how to fill six hours of time together. The good news is, working on team dynamics with the goal of aligning team performance to organisational outcomes is rarely if ever a wasted experience. I absolutely love it.

This book is not intended to be a textbook on team dynamics, so I will just share a few key concepts on the topic that I hope will support your thinking:

1. *Teams or groups have lifespans*
   Who hasn't heard of the concept of a team forming, storming and norming? Sometimes even conforming, or re-forming? This concept of group processes has been around for over 50 years, and was introduced by Bruce Tuckman in 1965.[20] In essence, each team that comes together, or is shaken up

---

[19] Griffin, E. et al. (2014). *A Field Guide for Organisation Development: Taking Theory into Practice*, 1st ed. Gower: London.

[20] Tuckman, B. W. (1965). 'Developmental sequence in small groups'. *Psychological Bulletin*, Vol. 63, No. 6, pp. 384–399.

by the loss of a member or gaining a new member, will go through a 'forming stage'. It is during this forming stage that people seek to understand each other, to determine each other's skills, behaviours and intent, and to make sense of how the group should work together toward a common goal. Even in the most harmonious of groups, a level of 'storming' will occur, in fact a complete absence of 'storming' can be indicative of a lack of challenge in the culture or even of group member apathy or false agreement, which is far more harmful to a culture than a spot of storming. So, we'll see people sizing each other up, potentially see people acting and responding as if they are threatened by another team member, and potentially overt conflict may arise. This 'storming' phase is a natural pathway of group and team development and is often compared to the teenage years of a human lifespan.

The 'norming' phase is when the common habits and ways of working of the group are formed – they have begun to know and understand how the group should operate together, and these are becoming cultural expectations of each other. It is during these early stages that an HR professional can advise or intervene to support healthy group functioning. It is also during these stages that an HR professional can support a leader to understand what the team is experiencing, what they may need to support them through each stage, and to ensure healthy norms are put in place that foster team cohesion and empathy.

I doubt this model is new to many of you reading this book. However, I often see new teams formed or restructures taking place without any real view to embedding these changes, or even creating processes to support new teams through the stages outlined above. This is where an HR person with an eye for team dynamics can come in and make a difference.

2. *Power dynamics in the workplace*

It is naïve to think that power dynamics don't matter, and your structure can be flat as the proverbial pancake; there will still be power dynamics at play. If we are seeking to treat people like people in the workplace, it is essential to understand how power works and to ensure it is used for positive intent, rather than to undermine or to disempower others. The concept of 'power blindness' is an interesting one for building a culture where people are treated like individuals, and where HR operates with 'heart'. I heard the term 'power blindness' from a colleague years ago and can't find a useful reference to share, but hopefully the idea of this will be useful to you in considering the power dynamics in your own organisation. It can be easy for any of us to be blind to the impact we have on others who have less power, status and privilege than us. Examples of this can be not replying to emails from those with less positional power than us or cancelling or regularly being late to meetings with people in lower status positions, as we're prioritising someone more senior for our time. As I write this paragraph, I'm reflecting on an instance just the other day when I was over an hour late for a phone-call with someone I hugely respect, but who admittedly was less senior in hierarchy to the person I had been held up in a meeting with. I had perhaps been caught up in my own power blindness. More overt examples include keeping closed within work social cliques and overlooking the power this gives members, for example sports social groups, or even the 'them' and 'us' groups that sometimes exist between fee-earners and support staff in large corporates.

Power dynamics are even at play when we use acronyms in front of people who won't understand them or arrange social events that exclude those who can't afford them or are unable to attend at certain times. Why is power blindness so important? Those with less power may be left feeling marginalised, overlooked, or unimportant, which can have a detrimental impact on employee engagement, performance and an individual's sense of self-worth. This is one example of how power impacts on group dynamics but demonstrates why we need to keep it at bay. Encouraging greater self and social awareness, and encouraging people to be inclusive in their behaviour, will minimise its impact.

3. *The dreaded Groupthink in our decision-making*
   We've all likely felt the need at some point to suppress our true ideals, beliefs and opinions to avoid entering into conflict, potential resentment, or perhaps to avoid feeling out-of-place. This often happens when we are debating beliefs or considering ideas or solutions to problems. Janis,[21] one of last century's most well-known psychologists, coined the term 'Groupthink' to account for the fact that groups high in uniformity or cohesion tend to make unanimous decisions without properly evaluating all possible options or by suppressing true individual opinions to avoid conflict. There are lots of examples of Groupthink in action, many of which have had dire consequences within public life and within organisations.

   Executive teams often think they are immune to this phenomenon because they are so cohesive, or because they offer each other challenge. It is important to observe what your teams are willing to challenge each other on though, and who challenges whom. Will the Exec challenge their CEO or Chair? Will they challenge on strategy or only on points

---

[21] Janis, I. L. (1982). *Group Think*, 2nd ed. Houghton Mifflin: Boston, MA.

of accuracy? Will they challenge if someone appears upset or distressed about their proposal being agreed? Putting the 'human' back into Human Resources isn't about supporting groups to be nice to each other. Yes, of course people should support and respect each other, but they should also be able and willing to constructively challenge to get to the right answer. Our role as HR colleagues is to hold a mirror up to reflect when this is not happening. Our role is also to challenge the organisation to embed the right governance and decision-making processes to protect against bias such as Groupthink.

I said there were many examples of Groupthink. It has been blamed for the ill-judged invasion and occupation of Iraq, the Volkswagen emissions scandal (among many other corporate issues), and of course the failure to forecast the financial crisis. How can we protect against Groupthink as HR professionals and partners to the business? First, we can ensure there is diversity of thought within our own teams and within our leadership teams. And we can introduce people of different backgrounds and styles of thinking or acting to the team and describe and role-model a culture of challenge. If you're not in the team itself, share the importance of constructive and trusting challenge, and help people to build the skills to feel confident in demonstrating this. And ensure incentive systems align with the long-term benefits of the organisation and are not conflicted with personal incentives of the team.

4. *Team cohesion and how we can achieve it*
   I have been using 'team' and 'group' interchangeably, and mainly because the biggest difference is that the former is really the latter with a sense of common purpose or a common goal. How far a group feels like a team, and feelings do matter in business, will have an impact on the

performance of that group of individuals. This is where the concept of 'team cohesion' can be helpful. Casey-Campbell and Martens (2009)[22] described team cohesion as the 'shared attraction or bonding among team members that is grounded in social- or task-based aspects of team membership, and that drives team members to remain together'. In the spirit of this definition, individuals feel part of a cohesive group when they like what the group stands for and feel a sense of shared importance of what the group achieve together. They suggest that team cohesion is a key contributor to team effectiveness and performance, and also to individual job satisfaction.

It will come as no surprise to you that people's experiences of work are often strongly affected by their experience of working within their immediate work team. If we can build strong work team cultures and a sense of pride in being part of a team, it would therefore suggest that we can build a strong and productive organisational culture. Furthermore, research suggests that cohesion plays a stronger role in performance than vice versa, or more simply put, if a team feels strongly connected to each other, they are more likely to perform better as a result. A high-performing group of individuals does not, however, make it more likely that you will build a cohesive team by bringing them together than a less high-performing group.

5. *Trust as the cornerstone of effective teamworking*
   Trust is a key part of any well-functioning relationship, whether in or outside of the workplace. For team members

---

[22] Casey-Campbell, M. and Martens, M. L. (2009). 'Sticking it all together: A critical assessment of the group cohesion–performance literature'. *International Journal of Management Reviews*, Vol. 11, p. 2.

to work together effectively, it is critical for them to trust one another. There are many definitions of 'trust' – Mayer and Davis (1995)[23] describe trust as the 'willingness of a (person) to be vulnerable to the actions of another (person) based on the expectation that the other will perform a particular action, irrespective of the ability to monitor or control that (person)'. When this expectation is shared amongst team members, it emerges as team trust. It's useful to know that we humans often equate trust with likeability. However, it's perfectly possible to like someone and to not want to trust them with your shiny new project or with getting to a high-profile meeting on time. You've got to believe the person is reliable and competent. Why is this concept helpful for HR professionals? Watch the dynamics in action within your client groups, and you will often see line managers (often new line managers) trying to be 'friends' with their direct reports, thinking or hoping that it will build stronger trust. However, this is not the most effective way to build long-lasting trust in a line management relationship. If the line manager wants to build trust, they will need to build others' perceptions of who they are, and their expectation for what they can do. Stephen R. Covey of *The 7 Habits of Highly Effective People* fame,[24] describes trust as 'the belief in who the person is, and a belief in their abilities'. A leader must literally practise what they preach, they should be transparent and

---

[23] Mayer, R. C., Davis, J. H. and Schoorman, F. D. (1995). 'An integrative model of organisational trust'. *Academy of Management Review*, Vol. 20, pp. 709–734.

[24] Covey, S. R. (2013). *The 7 Habits of Highly Effective People: Powerful Lessons in Personal Change*, 25th Anniversary edition. RosettaBooks: New York.

honest in their intent, and they should have the expertise to do their job. So, if you're advising your leaders on how to build a sense of trust within their teams, there is much more to it than group lunches and social nights out.

Amy Cuddy, the author of *Presence*,[25] introduces further key factors to support how we build and maintain trust. These factors are warmth and competence. Cuddy suggests that these two factors alone account for more than 90% of the variance in the positive or negative impressions we form of the people around us. Personally, I find it incredibly heartening to read of the potential importance that 'warmth' plays in building trust. From a selfish perspective, I spent the first five years of my 'career' being criticised for being high in warmth, or what I suspect people were referring to when they said that I was 'too nice to work in HR'. I remember a former boss laughing at me because I would genuinely shed a tear when someone got the promotion that they had been working so hard for. Cuddy isn't just describing happiness for others or showing concern and an interest in others though. Cuddy and her fellow researchers outline how warmth describes positive body language, generous actions and even smiling at others. So, watch your leaders in action, and remind them that being competent and tough-minded won't be enough to support them in building trust with their people and their customers.

Without getting too precious about it, it is for all the reasons outlined above that OD and behavioural science offer so much to the world of HR and how we can build people-centred workplaces. People are people and not paperclips, and this is a value set at the very core of OD. Whether we

---

[25] Cuddy, A. (2015). *Presence*. Orion Publishing Group: London.

develop deep knowledge as OD practitioners and consultants or operate as HR professionals with a keen interest in the field, hopefully the nuggets of OD knowledge shared in this chapter have whet your appetite to stay curious and to find out more. It's only through furthering our knowledge into how and why people behave as they do, and applying this in our workplaces, that we will create workplaces where people can thrive.

Toolkit D: Putting your OD glasses on

How can you continue to build your personal knowledge and skills in OD as an HR practitioner, and support this development of OD capability within your wider team? Some suggested steps follow in the toolkit below:

1. *Put your curiosity into action, and research the topic*
    OD differs from learning and development in that it doesn't focus exclusively on the organisation's staff – it also aims to influence processes, procedures and culture. Organisational Development is an interdisciplinary approach that draws on a variety of fields, including psychology, sociology, motivation theories and neuroscience. We've merely scraped the surface of the wealth of theory and knowledge in the field in this last chapter. I can't recommend the textbooks I've referenced any higher – I strongly suggest reading a few interesting chapters or articles and igniting your wider interest in the topic.

2. *Seek further development and/or mentoring support to support your practice*
    The key word here is 'practice'. OD is a skill set and requires continual practice. A book such as this, or even a more in-

depth OD book, will only take you so far in developing your OD capability. Attending a workshop on developing OD skills could be a hugely valuable investment for you or seeking coaching or mentoring support to work on certain aspects of your OD capability could be equally valuable.

3. *Working without judgement, with positive intent and curiosity*
   I held these up earlier in the chapter as being the true strengths or qualities of great OD practitioners. In exploring how far you are achieving or demonstrating these qualities, I would encourage you to consider the following questions by yourself or with your team:

   ○ *The role(s) you prefer to take on when working with others.* What role are you most comfortable in when working with your customers, and why?

   (Do you tend toward consultant, expert, helper, partner, humble enquirer, or another role altogether?)

   ○ *The impact of your role-taking on the dynamic with your customer.* How does your preferred role support or detract from your ability to facilitate an outcome with your customers, as opposed to leading or directing that outcome?

   (The relevance, of course, being that OD is about supporting and enabling people to create their own outcomes, as opposed to acting in expert mode.)

   ○ *Your needs within your stakeholder relationships.* What motivates you to achieve a great job for your customers, and why?

(Exploring why it matters to you is an important step to understanding the dynamic that can arise when these needs and motivations aren't met.)

○ *The power dynamic and broader dynamic at play.* What, if any, barriers are there to you having honest, direct conversations with your key stakeholders? If you knew you would be successful, how would you approach breaking down some of these barriers?

The questions above are designed to get you thinking about how you interact with others, and your own needs and motivations in those relationships. The importance of this self-exploration is that it can uncover patterns in how you relate or don't relate to others and is a useful and practical introduction to power dynamics within your real-life example.

I shared the concept of 'self as an instrument' with you earlier in this chapter. The purpose of reviewing and developing the knowledge, skills and mindset you bring to your practice will be key. This will be a continual process for you, and I find I continue to learn more about what my 'self' looks like through each new challenge or relationship in the workplace. Remember it's called 'dynamic' for a reason; relationships and how we and others experience them shift and change, as do our needs and motivations, so we can't expect to be done with honing our 'self as an instrument'.

Chapter 5

Systems thinking as an OD model, tool and mindset

Introduction

If I've seen one model turn on more lightbulbs in leaders' and HR professionals' minds than anything else, it is systems theory. In a nutshell, systems theory proposes that organisations are designed like systems, with each part of the system interacting to create the environment or culture of that system. The people milling about in our organisational system have their own individual personalities, values, motivations and needs, and, ultimately, they all interact together in a beautiful (and sometimes not so beautiful) dynamic that constantly changes. It's important to appreciate that if we are to create workplaces where people are motivated, and where high performance is most likely to occur, we need to intervene in a way that creates change across the system rather than in just one small piece of it. There are many models to illustrate systems thinking within Organisation Development, and there are numerous tools to put this into action in cultural change and organisation design programmes. Beyond models and tools, I have found that systems thinking is also a mindset. It is about seeking connectedness, and the desire to create sustainable change when there are often strong pressures to just focus and fix one component of the system.

It's no mean feat to achieve alignment across an organisational system. When that alignment is indeed achieved, external or internal influences will likely impact upon it and it's time to change again. As that old adage states: 'change is the only constant'. If that is indeed true, and it would certainly seem the case, we might as well get pretty good at changing. This is where OD and the study of human behaviour through occupational psychology really comes into its own. How can we possibly adapt and change without a strong understanding of how the core elements of our organisations respond to change – without understanding humans, how can we hope to support them through the ever twists and turns of organisational change?

How can systems thinking help us to solve organisational or cultural issues?

In my experience, systems thinking is most impactful when cause and effect just won't cut it any longer. Sometimes cause and effect works adequately, for example, when you're travelling, run out of petrol and your car stops. Your car stopped (effect) because it had no petrol (cause). If you put petrol in again, your car will run. Linear thinking is quite effective in solving this kind of problem, and we know what to do to get the outcome we desire. Systems thinking provides a perspective that, most of the time, various components affect each other in various, and often unexpected, ways. This is exactly what happens in organisations. It is rare to find linear thinking that can be applied reliably to a complex organisational problem, such as how to respond to a budget deficit or how to support greater cross-organisational collaboration and networking.

Adopting a systems approach takes persistence and curiosity, as you are seeking out novel answers to complex problems and seeking to really understand what you're observing. And this approach doesn't always come very naturally to people. We're taught to find solutions to problems and being 'decisive' is usually a description of someone who can very quickly find that solution and tell people what to do. Taking a systems thinking approach can infuriate those around you, who aren't interested in your exploration of the issue, and would like to see a 'quick fix' presented speedily for them to action. If you're seeking sustainable change though, and with finite resources and an organisational vision to achieve, why wouldn't you? I would suggest you start to develop your systems thinking muscles. One way to start to shift from linear to systems thinking is to practise identifying whether something is the problem or merely a symptom of something deeper. Linear thinking tends to focus on addressing surface-level behaviours – or symptoms. Unfortunately, making a symptom go away won't solve the problem. In fact, it may make things worse and cause effects in other parts of the organisation. A manager taking a systems thinking approach will work to understand the underlying problem before addressing any of the symptoms. Usually, if the true problem is solved, the symptoms will be eliminated as well.

How do you know if you're seeing the real underlying problem or simply a symptom of something deeper? Below are four clues that what you are experiencing is an indicator of a larger problem rather than the problem itself:

- The problem being stated feels too small or specific in comparison to the time and energy people are spending complaining about it. If people are spending a great deal of time moaning about the kitchens at work, it's either because the issue is acute, or because they are actually frustrated by another problem altogether.

- If people are complaining about something that they should be able to fix independently, but are doing nothing about, this suggests a bigger issue is at hand. Apathy in an organisation can rarely be solved by a quick fix.

- The problem is blamed on a certain individual. They leave, but the problems persist. This may well be due to custom and practice; people are now used to a particular way of working. More likely, however, there is a cultural issue that needs addressed here, and leadership changes alone won't change that.

- Problems seem to sprout up endlessly. Organisations that rely on reactive, quick-fix approaches to leadership often see one problem arise as soon as the last is dealt with. Most linear thinkers won't realise that the two issues are related. Meanwhile, the underlying dynamics fuelling the problems may fail to be addressed. Or when they are addressed, the solutions to these are often activities, such as 'we need more training' or 'we need to tell people what is expected of them', rather than seeking to explore the underlying culture and the issues that are interacting to cause the problem.

As an HR professional seeking to create sustainable change, and to form workplaces where issues are tackled openly, you might consider a few signs of 'quick-fix thinking' to watch out for:

- Leaders are looking for 'low hanging fruit'/quick fixes and action these – they want to be seen to be 'doing' something and are often celebrated for these behaviours.

- Knee-jerk reactions, born out of anxiety and learned helplessness, prevent systems thinking from having a chance to occur. Whilst systems thinking is not slow, it will require you to take a moment to consider the different variables that contribute to a situation.

- As we've been exploring in earlier chapters, curiosity is an essential quality or skill of an OD practitioner. An absence of curiosity is a typical sign of quick-fix, cause and effect thinking.

- Analysis paralysis is another sign of cause and effect thinking. People with this affliction aren't seeking more data to explore the organisation as a system, they are hoping something will jump out of the data set to solve the problem for them.

- Tribal behaviour within departments in an organisation can drive cause and effect behaviours. There is no time or energy for looking across the organisation and for making connections between common issues, as the individual departments are busy in competition mode and looking after their own interests.

Why does any of this matter in considering how we can 'put the human back into HR'? Bringing care and compassion into the workplace won't happen by accident. It happens by design, and it won't happen solely through embedding caring values and behaviours within people processes and practices. It needs to be worked through everything the organisation does. HR need to be leading discussions within their organisations to ensure structures, processes and systems empower rather than undermine the accountability and development of their people. For example, there is little point in having values-based recruitment and an empowering performance management system within a wider organisation that affords individuals little financial accountability for their areas, manages through strict hierarchy and allows little freedom of how and when people can work.

Designing organisations that are people-focused

In reality, HR departments tend to focus on tinkering around the edges of organisational change. I'm not firing arrows here; I've done the same myself. We talk about 'organisational change' but we're usually restructuring a small part of the system by moving a few jobs around or changing a few job titles. I have only worked in a couple of organisations that have undertaken a wholesale organisation redesign, that is, looking across the entire organisation as a system, with a view to redesigning all aspects of that system if required. Everything was up for grabs, and though it took a lot of organisation and a great deal of thinking, my goodness it was an empowering and refreshing way of working. There are a multitude of reasons for taking this approach, not least because it prevents a restructure from being mistaken as a 'design' effort. Restructuring under the guise of 'design' rarely goes beyond the 'tinkering' stage, and fails to ensure sustainable, impactful change. However, we don't always have the capabilities, energies or desire to take change to this level.

Why don't more organisations recognise the importance of strong organisation design to enable their strategy? My prevailing impression is that organisations either overlook the importance of organisational design, or simply don't know where to start. Whilst many HR Leaders hire experts in organisation design to support change, it's only in the larger HR teams that I've observed any designated organisation design resource.

The components of the organisational system

So, if we're exploring the organisation as a system to decide if it's fit for purpose or to determine if there is readiness for a key change, what components should we be seeking to explore? The components outlined below are from working with internal OD models in large government departments, but you might equally find that some OD consultancy models introduce a stronger focus on process redesign or a more detailed breakdown of 'ways of working'. The desired outcome is to support the development of a healthy organisation, and this requires ensuring all aspects of the organisational system are fit for purpose and aligned.

- *Strategy* – what is your strategic direction? How clear, achievable and compelling is it?

- *Structures* – what structures, hierarchies and spans of control exist within your organisation? Does this support your vision or detract from its success? For example, you may seek to be entrepreneurial but you have several lines of hierarchy and spans of control between someone and their ability to achieve this.

- *Governance and decision-making* – in reviewing your organisation design, you would typically map or collate all your governance and decision-making processes, reflecting on how these work in reality and, again, how this supports or detracts from your vision or desired outcome. Decision-making is a particularly interesting area. This is not only about how decisions are made, but by whom, and who is listened to in decision-making.

- *Leadership and management* – the leadership and management culture, the formal and informal networks for these groups, and how they are or are not called upon to support decision-making all play a key role in the effective functioning of an organisation. This can be explored through examining formal and informal communication mechanisms, and through speaking to employees about how they experience 'leadership' within the organisation. Survey data would be a good starting point, if you run one.

- *Ways of working* – 'ways of working' encompasses 'how things are done around here'. I believe it is often what people are talking about when they join a new team or organisation and talk about 'the culture'. When new joiners talk about having settled in, it is often because they have started to understand and adapt to new ways of working. This might include understanding the informal dynamic and conversation in the office or understanding the hotdesking system and how to book a desk. It might also be understanding how formal policies translate into reality, for example, the working hours state X to X in your contract, but in reality everyone leaves at 4:30 pm.

- *Behaviours (values and culture)* – is there alignment between what an organisation wants to achieve and the behaviours that are held up as being important to achieving that? For example, are the behaviours all about reliability, dependability and focus, when you need to focus on creativity, innovation and agility to achieve your vision? Ensuring strong alignment between the values and behaviours celebrated, recognised and communicated in your organisation will be key to achieving change.

- *Processes and systems* – your processes and systems will tell you a great deal about your culture, but also how fit for purpose your organisation is to achieve its strategy. In a fast-paced marketplace, your organisation might need to draw together multi-faceted project teams very quickly. This might lend itself to agile working, yet in fact your organisation uses archaic processes to support siloed working between teams, and relying on systems that don't support collaboration or communication between teams. Whilst the intent might be present and genuine, the systems and processes are acting as a constant barrier to achieving change.

Summary

There are so many things that OD can bring to the workplace and how we achieve great things with and for our people at work. Systems thinking is a source of real inspiration to me, and there are some amazing thinkers out there in the field of OD who would do the topic far greater justice than I. I just hope if they're reading this book, they are now doing so with a big dose of compassion and won't eat me alive for a less than fabulous portrayal of an incredible topic.

Moving on from exploring systems thinking and the design of people-centred organisations, it seems fitting to explore the values and leadership that will facilitate this change. Though only one aspect of the organisational design, the values and leadership in our systems have a huge impact on culture and how individuals experience their place of work. The next chapter will be devoted to one key value that I believe we should be keenly interested in as HR professionals: compassion. Through understanding compassion as a value, skill and behaviour, and seeking to adopt it in our own practices and as an organisational value, I believe we will create a movement toward greater humanity in our workplace.

Toolkit E: Piecing together your culture

This toolkit provides a basic, high-level guide for considering how far your team/organisation design is fit for purpose. It would be wonderful if you could reflect on your organisation design in the context of how you can develop a person-centred culture in HR and/or the wider organisation. After all, we're trying to shift toward a 'people not paperclips' culture.

1. *Articulating your case for change* – I shall grandly package your 'Why change?' reflections as your case for change. As discussed earlier, please don't leap over this stage, or assume that you're 'done'. The intended output is a series of statements, which outline why you are seeking to achieve a person-centred culture, and why now?

Try to step away from any soundbites and to seek to define what this change will mean for *your* organisation and *your* people. It will certainly help to pull together these reflections as a team or community within your organisation, as this will increase the diversity of thought informing your case for change.

2. *Determining your 'as is' position – 'where are you now?'* I've posed a series of questions aligned to each component of the organisational system for you to contemplate, and I would propose that you apply them to your own organisation with the question, 'How far is our team/ organisation design fit for purpose to achieve our strategy and vision?' This is no mean feat but will stand you in good stead for the next task in this toolkit.

3. *Where do you want to get to?* Early on in an organisation design project, you should be considering where you want to get to as an organisation, and the themes or principles that will guide you in designing this organisation system of the future. This isn't a set of values or behaviours, or a project plan of deliverables. What will guide you to achieve a person-centred culture? What are some of the principles that you sign up to as an organisation, and will adhere to as you consider structures, processes and practices in support of your strategy? Examples of design principles might be 'Flexibility', 'Putting benefactors at the heart of all we do', 'Removal of duplication of effort' or 'Inclusion'. Your choice of design principles guides what is important to you. It also supports you in assessing how far structural, process or behaviour activities will achieve a person-centred culture whilst staying true to these design principles.

4. *Bringing the outside in* – stakeholder engagement and influencing needs to be introduced from the outset of contemplating change, and before you have actually already decided what you want to do. When you know what you want to achieve and why, and your 'as is' and 'to be' analysis has supported you to consider the gap you will need to bridge to achieve that, it is another opportunity to engage with a wide set of stakeholders to understand change readiness and the appropriate pace of change. An important point to note as a change practitioner is that the process is just as important as the outcome. People will remember how they experienced a change process long after they've reconciled any negative feelings about the outcome of the change itself. So consult, inform and invite feedback whenever possible.

These are tips intended to support you in developing your OD mindset and diagnostic skills. The toolkit could become a whole change project in itself, so we will stop there, and move on to explore one aspect of the organisational system: the values and skills that will support a person-centred culture. In the next chapter we will focus on 'compassion', a value close to my heart.

Chapter 6

Leading our organisations with compassion

Introduction

Creating organisational cultures that are caring or demonstrate compassion to their employees will only become more important, as the people we recruit and want to retain are becoming increasingly savvy to the fact they should expect to be treated like 'people not paperclips'. Compassion involves an authentic desire to support others and to alleviate their suffering or discomfort. We know that the role of the emotional well-being of people has been often underappreciated and undervalued at work, and well-being has been put centre stage (or nearly centre stage) in the HR and management literature over very recent years. This is a good sign of course, but are we really seeking to make a step change toward more person-centred workplaces that treat people like humans with human needs? Or, are we perhaps just tinkering around the edges with some policies and practices that genuinely intend to support the ever-elusive 'employee well-being', but just never quite cut it? We need a holistic approach that seeks to create behavioural change. For example, there is little point in offering yoga before breakfast, mindfulness lessons at lunchtime, if people don't feel valued, respected and, dare I say, 'cared for' by their line manager.

When we treat ourselves and others compassionately, we tend to come together in a contributory manner that raises the group to greater heights as a whole. With this, bonds are formed, trust is established, and a willingness to collaborate on projects and shared visions becomes the driving force behind our intentions. Whilst empathy is putting ourselves into the shoes of another person, and seeing the world through their eyes, compassion takes this a step further. Compassion is about caring for another's experience and taking action to alleviate their suffering. It is all too easy to read about others' suffering in the newspaper or to notice someone struggling at work and do nothing. There is a whole body of work on bystander apathy and diffusion of responsibility – in short, we assume someone else will do something.

The perception of misperception of compassion at work

Little things make a big difference. An old colleague once gave out 'free hugs' at Waterloo station on behalf of our previous employer, a national charity. Whilst not everyone wanted a hug at the station, the offer of connection gave joy to at least a few folks as they battled public transport that day. In a busy world, time out to connect with others is increasingly important. Such acts of kindness as a 'free hug' or making a colleague a cup of tea are a fantastic starting point for building a culture where we look out for the needs of others. If it's not clear now that I couldn't be more passionate about the need for compassion and care in the workplace, it will be by the end of this chapter. I was told on a number of occasions in my early career that I'm 'too nice'. There was an undertone to these suggestions that wasn't lost on me. Displaying compassion and empathy were somehow viewed as weak, and I needed to show greater emotional detachment at work. I wasn't offering free hugs in the canteen – I was merely demonstrating care and concern for those around me. In a further assertion of defensiveness, I would label my behaviour in these instances as 'kind' and not 'nice'. I've since come to find that compassion to others, whether through small acts of kindness such as Sue Ryder's 'free hugs' or through getting to know people as individuals, isn't weak at all. I can be compassionate toward others whilst still offering supportive challenge and holding others to account. In fact, I'm often the person championing the need for courageous conversations. Workplaces can be kind and courageous.

I've also worked within workplaces where process regularly takes precedence over the needs of people; any action is condoned as long as the end outcome is achieved. Such cultures are unhealthy and are fraught with cultural issues that aren't sustainable for long-term success. The research stacks up in favour of kind workplaces to drive high performance and engagement. An important connection has been found between compassion in teams and ongoing team connection and performance (Frost et al., 2000),[26] and a strong link between compassionate leadership and high employee engagement (Lilius et al., 2008)[27]. *People care that we care.* So, what little things can we each do as HR professionals, and as organisational citizens to role-model compassion at work?

- *Make an effort to get to know people* – ask others if they had a good weekend and take the time to actually listen to the answer. Take the time to introduce yourself to new people at work. It's only superficial if you don't genuinely want to get to know the other person.

---

[26] Frost, P. J., Dutton, J. E., Worline, M. C. and Wilson, A. (2000). 'Narratives of compassion in organizations'. In S. Fineman (ed.) (1993). *Emotion in Organisations.* Sage: London, pp. 22–45.

[27] Lilius, J., Worline, M., Maitlis, S., Kanov, J., Dutton, J. and Frost, P. (2008). 'The contours and consequences of compassion at work'. *Journal of Organisational Behaviour*, Vol. 29, pp. 193–218.

- *Lead by example in displaying compassion, no matter what 'level' of the organisation you're employed at* – offer help and support to others, and condolences when they're going through a hard time. This creates a ripple effect of kindness. People who are treated with kindness, often seek to 'pay it forward' and to offer kindness to others in return.

- *As a leader, role-model compassion as an organisational value to aspire to* – Melwani et al. (2012)[28] found that people who act compassionately are perceived to be stronger leaders. Great leaders lead from the heart and inspire others through kindness and support.

- *Make space for informal connection* – don't allow yourself or your team to exist in a 'busyness trap', so busy on a treadmill of 'doing' that we think we don't have time to stop and chat. Yes, certainly get your work done, but think of a 'chat' as a connection instead of wasting time.

- *Invite more authenticity and open communication in the workplace* – allow for honest and open debate, act without judgement and respond to issues with curiosity: an issue needs to be explored, not 'acted' upon.

- *Welcome and celebrate compassionate behaviour* – it demonstrates the value placed on these behaviours and provides greater meaning for people at work. I've recently left a role at the National Physical Laboratory where 10% of the workplace are trained as Mental Health First Aiders, trained and able to support their colleagues in times of

---

[28] Melwani, S. et al. (2012). 'Looking down: The influence of contempt and compassion on emergent leadership categorisations'. *Journal of Applied Psychology*, Vol. 97, p. 6.

mental distress. Each person was publicly and privately thanked for their contribution. I was blown away by how motivated people were to make a difference to the lives and experiences of others.

- *Keep perspective* – there are times when command and control are needed in the workplace, but I have rarely worked in a workplace where the nature of the work demands this. We nearly always have time for exploring concerns with others.

- *Leave your ego at the door* – no matter your craft, leave your ego at the door and respect the contribution of all those around you. You're never too senior, too 'expert' or too 'busy' to show care and compassion to others.

The above tips and techniques will support you in role-modelling compassion in your workplace. Acting with compassion is something we need to openly encourage and practise daily, and we need to challenge where this doesn't take place. It will be interesting to explore with your teams how they believe you are individually and collectively bringing compassion into the workplace.

Leading with humanity: compassion as a core value

Early in his book, *Compassionate Leadership*, Hopkinson[29] writes: 'A Compassionate Leader starts their understanding at home. Look in the mirror first: Who are you? How are you? Really? Be honest.' His point is that once people have a true understanding of themselves, they can gain a better understanding of others

---

[29] Hopkinson, M. (2014). *Compassionate Leadership: How to Create and Maintain Engaged, Committed and High-Performing Teams*. Piatkus, imprint of Hachette UK: London.

and so create more effective business and personal relationships. Hopkinson draws on five qualities that he considers to be the basis of compassionate leadership:

- *Awareness* – self-awareness is key to self-compassion and to offering compassion to others.

- *Courage* – the courage to be authentic, regardless of the circumstances.

- *Confidence* – this is the self-belief that 'you can and will make it work', which could also be referred to as resilience when under pressure.

- *Joy* – Hopkinson believes that the modern world encourages people to focus on the destination rather than the journey, and compassionate leadership requires joy in the process.

- *Compassion* – in essence, Hopkinson says compassion is 'having the peripheral vision to see others and help them along the journey of awareness, courage, confidence and joy'. Hopkinson draws a distinction between empathy and compassion: 'Empathy is a desire to know the other person. Compassion is to act on that knowledge with positive intent.'

Compassionate leadership is not about being 'nice' all of the time – it is about having a strong awareness of your own sense of self, being confident and courageous in sticking to your core values and acting to support people to achieve their own sense of purpose and well-being. It is no surprise that there are some leaders who will operate with scant consideration or compassion for others, perhaps showing indifference and apathy for individuals ('I need to make £1 million, so I need to hire ten people, that is, individuals don't matter, they are a means to an end') or they put their own egos above their team ('I need people to make me look good'). The best leaders are those who lead from the heart, those who have the ability to inspire others through kindness, flexibility, support and empowerment. When you treat people with compassion they never forget and, as a result, you develop people who want to work for you because you care. I came across a fantastic research project a while ago from the talented researchers at Roffey Park. Meysam Poorkavoos[30] conducted research on compassion and work with Roffey Park in 2016 and designed a Compassion at Work Index (CWI) to profile compassionate leadership traits. I particularly love this research because it breaks 'compassion' down into five core areas, which illustrates perfectly why compassion really isn't 'soft' or 'fluffy'. The areas the CWI focuses on are:

1. *Being alive to the suffering of others* – being sensitive to the well-being of others and noticing any change in their behaviour.

2. *Being non-judgemental* – not judging others and validating their experience.

3. *Tolerating personal distress* – the ability to bear others' distress – it doesn't overwhelm to the point of preventing action.

4. *Being empathic* – understanding the sufferer's pain and feeling it as if it were one's own.

5. *Taking appropriate action* – taking appropriate action to support the sufferer.

---

[30] Poorkavoos, M. (2016). *Compassionate Leadership: What Is It and Why Do Organisations Need More of It?* Research Paper: Roffey Park.

Applying compassionate leadership in our organisations

We've explored what we can each do to practise greater compassion at work, and we've explored the research that underpins why we should care about taking this action. How can we encourage greater compassion in our leaders?

- *Share the story* – tell people why this matters: give examples, research or case studies, whatever the best hook is for your audience. Tell the story of why this isn't 'soft' and why it's not the realm of HR departments. People remember being cared for by their organisation when they need it most, and it keeps these people in the organisation and motivated to give their best.

- *Seek role models* – take some of your best talent who demonstrate high performance and high compassion and roll them out time and time again to tell the story above. They are your storytellers. Apparently, we need to hear the same thing repeatedly to remember it. (Three times? Seven times? I'm not sure we need to know here, but it's multiple times.) So, tell the story again and engage people, ask them if and how they relate to it, and find a 'type' of care and compassion that fits the needs of your culture and your people.

- *Challenge where you see a lack of compassion* – we need to hold people to account for delivering work outcomes in a way that is inclusive, collaborative and supportive to others. It is important that you challenge others where you see a lack of compassion (appropriately and sensitively, of course). And give this book to them to show why this stuff is so important in creating an environment where people can do their best work. Compassionate leadership calls for curiosity, listening and making adjustments in style or approach to meet the needs of individuals. Nevermind what their MBTI type is,[31] it might be quite a step change for the JFDI[32] leaders out there to change their approach. So, it's unrealistic to expect to give people the business case for this and to see behavioural change.

- *Explore compassion as a value, a behaviour and a strength* – compassion wears multiple hats. Yes, it's a value. Yes, it's a behaviour. But importantly it's also a strength that may or may not energise people. This is relevant because we can all overplay our strengths.[33] A strength of mine is compassion but in overdrive this can look like wanting to save people. People usually don't need me to save them; part of compassionate leadership is supporting people to 'save' or to act in their own best interests. It's important to explore the nature of compassionate behaviour and what it means to us individually, and to your leaders, so they can have the same level of awareness. Recognising how my compassion can go into overdrive offers me the opportunity to look at triggers for this behaviour and to tackle my own behaviour when it goes awry.

---

[31] A psychometric tool by the test provider, Myers Briggs International. Have a Google if you've managed to bypass it in the workplace.

[32] Just ****ing do it. Those leaders who expect a click of their fingers to achieve results. We've all worked for one.

[33] I would urge you to refer to the fantastic work of Paul Brewerton and his organisation, Strengthscope, in the area of strengths-based leadership. One of their core organisational values is 'changing lives' because they believe in sustainable change through their work. Inspiring.

Summary

'Leadership' and 'compassion' have not historically been words you would associate with each other. We often talk about people being pragmatic, decisive and objective as core management and leadership traits, and expect that people must be 'tough' to be able to make it to the top of their profession. I am often reminded of a line from the film *Cinderella*, which I must have watched hundreds of times with my young daughter. Cinderella is told to always 'have courage and be kind', which is wonderful advice in itself, but I would suggest it does in fact take courage to be kind. In a world that still celebrates toughness and where acting with kindness at work can still leave people being perceived as a 'soft touch', I think it can take true confidence and courage to develop a culture of care and compassion. I worked with a fantastic Group Captain at the Royal Air Force who recently told me about a time when he showed flexibility and care to someone in his team returning from a period of leave. He reflected that he was perceived as 'soft' after taking this decision but had to do the right thing. It took courage to stand out from the crowd and to be defined by a quality or value that others may not see as a strength. Compassion is often seen as the response of the naively kind-hearted, detracting from the need for robust, objective decision-making. I would counter that I can be both robust and objective whilst operating with compassion, and thankfully the workplace is shifting toward this mindset too.

Most of my coaching conversations, and the key workplace issues I have dealt with, have been due to poor communication or to unhealthy feelings that have not been addressed at work. Whilst compassion may still feel 'nice to have' as a key leadership trait, the reality is that most great leaders do make time for their people, and express compassion and regard for their feelings and experiences at work. Great leaders care about connecting with the people they lead, and it is compassion alongside empathy that enables them to do this.

Toolkit F: On compassionate leadership?

We're going to shift the toolkit back to focusing on you as a practitioner for this topic. How can you take small steps to reflect on yourself as a compassionate leader? Each person differs in the way they choose to show compassion to others, but you will find a series of tips, techniques or considerations for demonstrating compassionate leadership below:

1. *Practise mindfulness (or being present with others) to support compassion*

   It is not unusual for leaders to be caught in a busyness trap, potentially too busy to even ask people how they are, or perhaps to stand still long enough to hear and respond to the answer. This tip goes further though – if we want to be compassionate, we need to seek to understand the situation of an individual and to contemplate what 'action' we can take to support this. Compassion is not a passive game, so it is important that leaders seeking to practise compassion are mindful and willing to be present in the moment to listen to, and really hear, the thoughts and perspectives of their people.

2. *Create space to build and maintain trust*

   A compassionate leader never stops asking questions or seeking to give and receive feedback in their teams. This stems from the traits of curiosity and empathy that we have already explored but also a basic willingness to create space to continually work on the trust between them and their teams or stakeholders. Trust is not static; we continually give and receive trust based on our connections with others. Compassionate leaders will make the time to get to know people and will reflect on the trust they hold with these people, and how open they believe people are willing to be in sharing their issues or concerns.

3. *Embrace the 'action' that embodies a compassionate mind*
   This is not about saving others. In fact, I would suggest in many circumstances a leader should definitely not step in to solve the problems of their team members. Embracing action is putting yourself in a mindset where you are continually seeking to adapt your style, approach or activity to support and benefit others. People who are not suffering from physical or mental illness that prevents it are generally pretty well-equipped to support themselves. Your role is to empower, to guide and to signpost to resources that will support them.

4. *Build your ability to sit with your own discomfort to be there for others*
   Controlling my compassion in overdrive has long been a development need of mine, and I noticed this is one of the key components of Roffey Park's compassionate leadership model, coined 'tolerating personal distress'. People who feel overwhelmed by another person's distress may simply turn away and may not be able to help or take the right action. In HR, where we are privy to challenging information and we are driving forward a person-centred culture, we must be there for others without leaping into their problems with them.

Sometimes it's easy to forget that we need to be able to sit with difficult emotions in order to fully be there for others. This doesn't mean that we don't feel for others and their suffering, but we're able to sit with that discomfort to be present and there for another person in the moment. I was a Samaritans listener for a few years, and this is a value and skill that those very special volunteers on the end of the phone, email or webchat draw on to be there for people in emotional distress. The Samaritans has a vision to reduce suicide, and the Samaritans volunteers are likely to hear some very challenging stories from those needing their support. They are able to sit with their own discomfort, to be there for the person making contact, and will then be supported by their fellow volunteers afterwards. The feelings of empathy will always be there, but they do not override the person's ability to be there for the person contacting the Samaritans.

These are a few tips for getting into a compassionate mindset. You will find a wealth of resources to delve deeper into the topic from the writers and researchers referenced throughout this chapter. And you're probably doing much of this stuff anyway. If so, just get others to do it too, and hopefully we'll have a ripple effect of compassionate leadership throughout our workplaces.

SECTION THREE

LEADING AN HR SERVICE WITH HEART

Chapter 7

Rebranding the HR team

Introduction

I'm not sure how I feel about the term 'rebranding' as it sounds pretty painful. It also suggests that some sort of 'branding' happened in the first place. Typically, HR teams and others' perceptions of these teams grow organically with little concerted thought into 'What do we want to be known for?' and the 'brand' unsurprisingly is based on the reputation of the team/persons within HR, which in turn is influenced by what the business believes an HR service should look like. If we're to be successful in creating workplaces where people are valued and treated like individuals, we need to ensure our teams are known for this and that our end-to-end service reflects this. The next chapter will focus on what you as an individual HR professional can bring to the party. In this chapter, we will focus on the higher-level HR service. How do we ensure we're known as people-centred leaders who are leading people-centred teams, alongside the myriad of other hats we wear?

How we choose to work with our client groups

There are a number of 'things' we might be known for within HR.

We can be the *business partner*, who aims to contribute to change through understanding the business and its needs and applying HR knowledge and best practice to achieve this.

We can be the expert, bringing specialist expertise to support leaders and managers in making key business decisions, or in interpreting HR policy and practice. It's a traditional view of HR but it's an important one, as we rely on specialist knowledge in complex fields such as employment legislation and case law to protect and support our organisations.

As I write this, the focus within HR is on the 'strategic generalist', who works alongside specialists either internally or externally to enable the people strategy of their organisation. The 'Business Partner' term is not a new one in HR and reflects the importance of HR being seen as a 'key enabler to the business. Some futurologists, or perhaps just people in the know, have proposed that we will see a shift back to the core role of HR as being 'specialists' in the future and many of the generalist functions will cease to be of importance. HR admin and coordination, still a huge burden to many HR teams, will be supported by ever-increasingly sophisticated technologies, and the remit of HR will be to provide specialist knowledge and advice.

With a potential shift toward 'HR as specialist', we may see new HR roles created in the future. We may see an increased focus on the behavioural scientist within HR, and greater investment in specialist expertise to guide informed decision-making. We may see HR as a connector and strategist being of ever greater importance in the workforce. The reality is that we can make these predictions, but we don't know what the future will bring for HR. We do know that the closer we can get to understanding the businesses in which we work, and to challenging the business to create meaningful employment experiences for human beings, the more likely it is that we will be driving strategic impact in the workplace. This could mean that holding the capability and the drive to operate as a change agent, could be more important than ever to HR. A change agent is a driving force of change within a business and seeks to continuously improve how the organisation works toward its vision. Let's explore this particular buzzword in a little more detail, and some of the steps you can take to operate in this role yourself.

Exploring the role of 'change agent' in HR

David Ulrich, the guru of all things HR, has been saying for many years that HR needs to act as a change agent within organisations.[34] The HR team need to be role-modelling and championing change; we need to be spotting opportunities for change within the organisation and showing others how to make change happen. Gone are the days of being told 'we need to restructure' and facilitating an HR process in response. HR teams nowadays are hugely adept at partnering with the business to shape people capacity and capability in response to internal and external demands. However, the concept of 'change agent' takes this even further. We need to instigate the change and show others what is possible with the most precious part of the business (note, I didn't call people 'assets' here – we're people, not buildings).

As we've explored in earlier chapters, I'm not convinced we can 'manage change'. We can try to control a few variables around it, but ultimately change is a little like energy that ebbs and flows through an organisation. Change is not a project or programme of work that has a defined start and finish date, and change can't be reduced to a set of KPIs ticked off by the senior leadership teams. We've already explored how HR can role-model the importance of taking a systemic, person-centred approach to

---

[34] Ulrich, D. (2012). *HR from the Outside In: Six Competencies for the Future of Human Resources.* Amacom, sub-imprint of HarperCollins Leadership: Nashville, TN.

organisational change, but there are also a number of ways HR can step into 'change agent' mode to kick-start change:

- *Practise what you preach and build a vison* – build a vision for what you want to create and talk to people about it. A vision is no good on a PowerPoint deck, rolled out for management meetings, but needs to become part of the conversations within the organisation and an aid for people seeking to visualise where the organisation is heading and why.

- *Stop thinking of yourself as a 'support function' or 'enabler'* – HR wears both of these hats of course, but to don the 'change agent' hat, you will need to stop thinking of how you can respond to business issues, and start thinking about how you can proactively create opportunities and shape the organisation for the future. If you have an entrepreneurial spirit, this will hopefully spark a sense of freedom and creativity in you. If you don't, these are muscles you can build and flex, and we'll explore that in the next chapter.

- *You are the change agents, not the function* – I don't want to steal the glory of the next chapter, but it is essential that you recognise that you in HR are individuals too. You are the change agents, and not the function. Sure, the whole is greater than the sum of its parts (thank you, Gestalt), but ultimately, we need to individually take ownership for creating change and role-modelling change through ourselves. As Malcolm Gladwell describes in his book, *The Tipping Point*, 'the success of any kind of social epidemic is heavily dependent on the involvement of people with a particular and rare set of social gifts'. It ultimately comes down to each of us contributing as positive agents of change.

- *Be in it for the long game* – being a change agent is not about rocking up, throwing in a few cultural curveballs, and making an overnight impact. You'll often be up against a sea of cultural barriers and these will have a bearing on the impact you can create and the speed in which you can achieve that. Be kind to yourself – contrary to what I just said above, it's not all about you. Creating sustainable change requires both patience and persistence. Most people need to experience something before they really understand it, and this will take time to take people on that, dare I say it, 'journey'. Being persistent isn't about chipping away at people until they agree with you; it's about remaining clear on your evidence-based vision and strategy, and continually working on how you achieve that based on the feedback and responses of those around you. Change agents need some humility; you're not always going to get it right and you need to stay adaptable.

- *Practise supportive challenge* – Ask the challenging questions of yourselves and others to kick-start change in the right direction. Keep asking questions to help people think, and don't be tempted to switch into expert mode through telling them what to do.

Being an ambassador for change – demonstrating people-focused leadership

Whether you lead the HR or OD team, or are a business leader accountable for people, you are or need to be an ambassador for creating a people-focused culture. Our aim to create cultures of 'people not paperclips' will not be born out of HR processes and values on the wall. There is no better place to start role-modelling and championing a people-centred culture than within the HR team (though the executive team would probably share the top spot).

We'll explore in the next chapter how everyone within HR can operate as trusted advisors and supportive 'helpers' to create change within organisations. But how can you lead in a way that promotes people as people, and that tells a story about the powerful impact of treating people like humans within individual needs at work?

1. *Connect with people and their needs in a truly human way* – find your connection with the organisation and its people that allows you to authentically, genuinely, wholeheartedly, care. This isn't a 'fake it until you make it' game. You may find that you particularly connect with seeing individuals thrive and achieve their potential within the workforce, or in seeing people's mental health being supported in a positive, inclusive way. Care for everyone as individuals, but don't be afraid to find your niche and to demonstrate your care and compassion through that for people. You will find that many people build trust through observing people treat others well, and trust in people who have a clear passion to make others' lives more fulfilled.

2. *Lead individuals, not 'people'* – instead of managing a workforce with a one-size-fits-all approach, consider that you are leading a 'workforce of one' with unique needs and motivations, and tailor your approach and your vision for success accordingly.

3. *Show humility* – leaders with a strong people focus behave like humans. They show vulnerability and admit when they have made a mistake. Humility has long been considered a key leadership strength, but it's not always one we see practised by senior leaders. We can shift this trend within HR, showing the importance of demonstrating humility in our approach and in our dealings with others. As a small

action, admit when you get things wrong, which will inevitably happen from time to time, and say sorry.

4. *Don't hide behind data* – build your evidence-base and seek long-term impact from your people strategies and interventions, but don't hide behind the data. Cultures are built on stories and informal dynamics. As a people-centred leader seeking to create change, you need to get under the skin of these stories to understand how you can better align them to your vision for the future.

5. *Use your knowledge of human behaviour or tap into the expertise of others* – people-focused leaders of the future need to utilise the tools and insights of a scientist to inform their business and people decisions. We need to understand what makes people tick, and how we can best motivate and retain the people who will support the organisation to be successful in the future.

6. *Work with a sense of purpose and share your personal values* – it's wonderful to feel aligned to your organisation's values, but don't forget to share your personal values and to connect with others on a personal level. Working with a clear sense of purpose will be motivating for you, I hope, but it will also clearly indicate to others how you intend to create people-focused change. As Simon Sinek famously says, 'Why would anyone want to be led by you?' Don't leave them guessing and share this openly and generously with others.

7. *Communicate transparently and as much as possible* – by 'communicating as much as possible', I don't mean constantly giving people information with little tailoring to the needs of the audience. Communicate with the organisation, with teams and with individuals, and keep speaking to people across all levels of the organisation. Build an open and

collaborative partnership with your trade union, if you work with one, and demonstrate that your intentions and vision for the future are built on treating people with trust and respect.

8. *People-centred isn't the same as 'people are always right'* – people will do things at work that aren't appropriate, and that don't demonstrate trust and respect to others. People will sometimes be let down by the organisation, and they will have a right to explore this and for the situation to be remedied in an appropriate way. It is important that we are clear that people-focused leadership relies on creating a culture of trust and respect, and that this also involves holding others to account for supporting this too. Performance issues or poor behaviour needs to be tackled in a way that respects the individual, but also sends a clear signal that all people across the organisation are accountable for supporting a culture where people are treated like individuals. We need to demonstrate fairness in our approach, and this doesn't mean one rule for one person, and one rule for another.

9. *Know your people* – certainly, this gets trickier in large organisations or within distributed teams, but show a concerted effort to know who your people are and what they're known for.

There are many actions you can take to explore and define how you are currently perceived as an HR team, and to consider what you would like your brand to 'look and feel like' in the future. We will explore some of these potential actions or reflections in the toolkit at the end of this chapter.

Summary

In this section, following our foray into OD and compassionate leadership, we have explored how you can develop your team brand and what your HR team wants to be known for. This has supported us to also consider what 'people-centred' might mean within our organisations, and what it perhaps shouldn't mean. In summary, I would propose that being person-centred is about treating people with dignity and respect, and as individuals with individual needs and motivations. It isn't about doing whatever people say or want you to do or failing to set expectations and boundaries out of misplaced kindness. The toolkit that follows provides a framework for you to explore and build your team brand within HR; your starting point, what you want to collectively be known for, and how you might bridge any gap that exists.

Toolkit G: How can you influence and shift what you're known for as an HR team

First, I will suggest that you need to know what 'others', or at least a key subset of 'others', really think about your HR team. When you have this feedback, you can consider what the organisation needs from your team, and how you can reflect on the feedback and the vision for the future to create a powerful sense of where you need to head, and how. I have no doubt you'll be doing this in a context that is busy and requires a strong operational focus, that is, actually paying people, recruiting people and managing people issues. I've never spent a day with a team facilitating these conversations that have felt it was a waste of time – these conversations and the plan that evolves from them can drive a powerful step change for your team.

- *What is your team currently known for?*
Seek feedback from key stakeholders, those you wouldn't usually go to for feedback, and some of the potentially 'hidden' voices in your organisation. I respect that you're not conducting PhD-worthy research here, but do try to create a broadly representative sample, and do think about the number of people you need and want to approach. It would be helpful to understand how these people view the customer focus, leadership, style, and approach of your team. How would they describe how the team drive and/or support change, how responsive are the team, and what more could the team do or do differently to support organisational and leadership success?

- *Considering what's possible – what could you be known for?*
I'm hoping, given our work so far in this book, that creating a shift toward a people-centred workplace will be high on the list, as would facilitating sustainable change. It sometimes helps if you're not working from a blank sheet of paper when considering what you want to be known for. Consider with your team what else you might you be known for:

  o Is it for having a strategic focus; understanding your organisation and the sector it operates in, having a business focus and applying this to a robust people strategy?

  o Is it for having a strong operational focus; offering an HR service that gets the work done, that is responsive and operates professionally and in line with best practice?

  o Is it for building relationships; winning through customer intimacy, culture and employee engagement?

Spend some time painting a picture, whether using words, diagrams or indeed a picture, to illustrate what your team will look like in a year, two years or another timeframe that feels meaningful to the group. If your team tend to be 'visual', that is, find it easiest to work with information when they can see it and perhaps draw it, then draw a picture. If they like to write things down, to reflect on these words and to create a story to engage with, then write a story or a description of the future. One of my favourite ways to create a compelling, meaningful vision of the future is to write out what you with see, feel and experience in X years' time. For example:

'In two years' time, my team will be engaging readily with all levels of the organisation; people will be seeking their advice and there will be enthusiastic discussions as they share advice and create solutions together with their client groups. People will be saying that the team are credible, interested and interesting to work with. They will be respected for their knowledge and expertise, relationship-building skills and ability to build trust rapidly. They are role-modelling a person-centred culture, and people feel great trust in an HR department that cares.' Just an example for you.

* *How can you make this happen?*
  Your team should brainstorm this together – bringing in multiple viewpoints and diversity of thought is more inclusive and will develop a stronger outcome. Given the potential gap in the current perceptions of stakeholders and team members, and the compelling vision you have painted for the future, what needs to happen to create a shift toward that vision? What do you need to individually and collectively create, think,

feel and do to support this shift? There may be some individual capability that needs to be addressed in making the required shift, and it is likely that there will also be some behavioural shifts. You should be prepared that you may need to make some of these shifts yourself, and you should seek open and honest feedback from the team and stakeholders to ensure you understand what is needed.

The steps outlined above could be approached through a series of discussions or workshops with you and your team. The temptation can be to schedule an 'away day' so that you can work through all the topics during a single day. I would urge you to take more time if you can, and to allow for learning and reflection as you move between the different parts of developing 'what you want to be known for'.

Chapter 8

Putting 'the human' back into your individual HR practice

Introduction

In this chapter, we will move beyond the 'team brand' to focus on you. We are going to explore what *you* want to be known for as a leader and as an HR professional. We will also explore an important concept in the world of HR, that of becoming or being a 'trusted adviser'. The term is often used by consultancy firms to demonstrate their client focus, but it is equally useful when operating as an internal consultant or within an HR team. Trust, as Patrick Lencioni notes in his infamous book *The Five Dysfunctions of a Team*, sits as the core foundation of building a positive and effective team and a positive and effective workplace culture.[35] The skill and ability to build trust with others also sits as the foundation of a successful HR professional. The value of workplace trust cannot be overestimated. It's the foundation for collaboration, integrity and innovation. As such, it's the foundation for how we engage people.

---

[35] Lencioni, P. M. (2002). *The Five Dysfunctions of a Team: A Leadership Fable*. John Wiley & Sons: New Jersey.

Considering what you want to be known for as an HR professional

Ultimately, you're an individual, and putting aside all the buzzwords we explored in the last chapter, you need to decide what you want to be known for as an HR professional, and why. The reason I'm advocating time for reflection on this point, is that it will ultimately drive how you respond to tasks, activities and people within your role, and will, in turn, drive how others respond to you. I have advocated the need to be known for enabling and creating change and being someone who genuinely cares for the individual experience of people as human beings at work. There's clearly a choice for you there, but I would predict that you probably wouldn't have got this far in the book, or perhaps even opened it, if you weren't on board with those two proposals.

People may reflect on what they 'want to be known for' when looking for a new job, or perhaps when forced to reflect on their future as part of a leadership development programme or workshop. Most, however, will find scant time to reflect on this at all. First, it's important to note that when we're considering what you want to be known for or your 'personal brand', we are not talking about what your status is within the organisation or what your job title is. Your job title gives an indication of what you 'do', it doesn't tell the story of what you do that makes you different from the millions of other people with your job title, and it doesn't tell a story of the impact you create through being unique 'you'. People with a strong sense of what they want to be known for, they understand the value they create for and with others, and they both have a clear sense of personal purpose and a clear vision for the outcomes they want to see from their leadership.

What you want to be known for needs to be realistic, or at least planned out in some way. If you want to be known for creating new advances in medicine, and you currently work in merchandising for a clothes manufacturer, you are looking for a rather hefty career move that goes beyond the remit of this current chapter. However, what you want to be known for should be aspirational and inspire you to want to grow and develop.

Considering what you want to be known for starts with considering your personal values, beliefs and what is important to you. It is then that you can consider how you can authentically align these values and beliefs to create impact in your role as an HR professional. Let me give you an example from my own personal values and beliefs:

- I want to be known as someone who makes others feel valued, cared for and understood (*how I make others feel*).

- I want to be known for creating cultures where people can do their best work, and where each individual is treated with compassion, care and respect (*how I create outcomes*).

- I want to be known as a catalyst for change, seeking ways to create sustainable change within organisations that will support enduring positive gains in individual and organisational performance (*creating impact*).

- I want to be known for operating with fairness and with 'heart', regardless of the context or the issue I am attending to (*operating in line with my values*).

- I want to be known as an expert in the field of behavioural science and OD, forever learning but able to bring deep knowledge of the field to create impact at work (*recognition for my personal skills and expertise*).

Have a go at building your own personal brand, if you haven't done so already. To achieve this, you might want to ask others about how they perceive your strengths, where your talents lie and the difference you make. You can also reflect individually on questions, such as, 'What are my strengths and talents that I feel energised when I draw on?', 'Who do I impact or want to make a difference for?', 'What's important about this?', 'How do I do this?', 'What are my core values?' We'll explore this through some alternative questions in the toolkit at the end of this chapter.

Building trust as an HR Leader

HR is a consultative function, or it should be if we hope to 'partner' with our client groups and customers. An HR professional is no different from an accountant, management consultant or lawyer in that we carry high responsibility with little overt authority or final accountability for business decisions. It's not unusual for HR professionals to feel like they are 'going into battle' on behalf of people issues with the business, or potentially protecting the business from the disengagement or challenge of its people. It's not unusual to find HR professionals bemoaning their function as being like a 'policing' service or being a gatekeeper to tell employees 'no' to pretty much every request made that isn't explicit within a policy manual. I'm painting a pretty bleak picture and thank goodness there's been a marked shift from this picture in many organisations, but I would argue that the concept of HR being a 'trusted adviser' within an organisation is still a somewhat distant aspiration. The HR profession can state this as a professional aim, and run profession-wide capability building, but ultimately it will come down to the magical mix of skills and attitude sitting within an HR professional on the ground, in their exchanges with the business.

So, what is a 'trusted adviser', and how can you operate as one?

The key to operating as a 'trusted adviser' is, quite obviously, the ability to build trust with others. There are three parts to understanding trust and how we can build it; understanding how relationships operate, understanding the components of trust and understanding the process of trust creation. If this sounds complicated, it isn't, but remember that we're seeking to build our capability and skills based on an evidence-base and not a quick fix. So, bear with me, and we will explore how professional relationships tend to operate so that we can consider if building trust might look different within different work contexts and relationships.

Professional relationships operate at several levels:

- *Expertise-based-paradigm of giving answers* – this is a hugely tempting place to play, as we feel we are needed and that we have a certain status due to our expertise that others can't easily refute. It is also a risky place to play from the perspective of retaining HR talent in that it is easy to outsource pure 'answer-giving' advice.

- *Needs-based-paradigm of solving problems* – this paradigm is based more on asking questions to understand the problem. It comes from a deeper place of curiosity and shows greater partnering with the other person to diagnose and to respond to their problem. It is in this space that we saw the buzzword of 'value-add' spring up – it is assumed that there will be greater 'value-add' to the organisation if we are collaborating on understanding and diagnosing an issue with our business leaders or employees.

- *Relationship-based-paradigm for building trust* – in this area, your relationship with your stakeholder and the organisation goes beyond your job title or immediate area of expertise, and you are seen to be tailoring questions and solutions to the needs of the individual. This may seem like the domain of all good 'relationship builders' but too often we see relationship-building as 'do they like me' and 'am I reliable' as opposed to the additional merit of being seen to 'be building a relationship with the person as a human being'.

- *Trust-based-paradigm of building trust* – this is where the concept of our stakeholders as human beings really comes into its own. Our stakeholders don't come to find us during performance reviews or if there is a problem – they come to us for our insights and leadership regardless of the subject matter. I've shared this ultimate aspiration for building trust with my teams and others in the past, and it's sometimes provoked a reticent response. From delving deeper, it appears some reticence comes from the fact this feels a very personal approach, and not everyone has the appetite, time or inclination to build personal relationships with each and every stakeholder. I'd argue that's where you need to prioritise your time. We're not talking about building private relationships – not everyone wants to share their personal stories – but understanding what's important to someone and feeling like you know and understand that person is an important part of advising others.

What is trust, and how can we create it?

It is useful to distinguish between two types of trust:

- the trust that an organisation or person will do what they say they will, and is therefore reliable; and

- the type of trust that is built on an emotional connection that you know people will care and respond to you as a human being.

We often talk about the former type of trust when describing if we 'trust' a colleague. Will they be where they say they will be on time? Can I rely on them to work ethically and not to talk about me or my impact behind my back? Trust based on reliability is absolutely key to building a person-centred culture for obvious reasons, but trust based on connecting as human beings could be of even greater importance. The camaraderie we often observe within teams is a type of trust that goes beyond integrity and reliability and is based on believing that others have your back, and to use another colloquialism, they won't 'throw you under a bus' if things get difficult. For example, I may trust that my leader is reliable and consistent in their actions, but I still don't enjoy working with them because I feel they judge my issues and setbacks as personal failures, and they don't therefore 'have my back'. This isn't about leadership ignoring accountabilities and the inevitable mistakes and issues that take place, but it is about people feeling a shared sense of that accountability and a deep trust that their leader will do the right thing if tested. This is where the power of treating people like people, and not paperclips, is so incredibly important. It is this trust that so often does happen at team level – you'll see it in offices across the globe, in military teams on operation and when organisations come together to respond to a humanitarian crisis. It is the shared sense of purpose and trust that we are doing the right thing together that bonds us.

In exploring what a concept like trust 'is', it can be helpful to explore what it isn't. The opposite of trust is often observed as creating fear in others. Organisations that have high levels of trust tend to have a powerful sense of identity, which can be observed as a 'strong culture'. An organisation that builds trust amongst its employees operates from a platform of strength, therefore maintaining organisational resilience and motivating its people. In essence, trust-based teams perform, whilst fear-based teams are likely to be left spiralling in apathy. Fear creates aversion to risk, it creates feelings of nervousness and apathy within an organisation and its people, and it is the antidote to a person-centred culture. For all those leaders who feel it could be beneficial to invoke a spot of fear in its people, it is important to note that fear will never be an enduring motivator. Some of the simplest of motivation theories illustrate that fear is a 'hygiene factor' or a factor that people engage with to avoid pain. What are the risk factors for fear manifesting itself in this way within organisations? Fear breeds particularly well in command-and-control management structures, where ultimately people understand that their role is to do what they're told and on time. It is within such structures where, historically, people have been patted on the head and called 'a good pair of hands', which I believe is an effective euphemism for 'does what they're told'. Certainly, as we see in military leadership, there are times when command and control is absolutely vital, for example in a crisis situation when we need to coordinate and act rapidly. However, even in such a critical situation with high time pressures, we need to be able to trust that we can question actions that contravene ethics and values, and that we will be listened to.

Trust doesn't merely happen within one person, that is, it's not just about my reaction to you. Trust is the constant flow of interactions between people and, in this way, it is in a constant state of ebb and flow. The 'trust deficit', a term coined in occupational psychology, describes how the trust we hold with another person or indeed an organisation can be in excess or deficit, based on our ongoing interactions. If our trust goes into deficit due to a wrongdoing or a business decision we do not agree with, we seek to rectify this in some way, or sometimes through expecting something of the person or organisation to actively rebuild trust. This is an important concept in building person-centred organisations as it serves as a constant reminder that we need to continually work to create and maintain trust with each other, and with the people who work for our organisations. We can never take people for granted or assume they will agree with our actions and decisions. Through treating people like human beings at work, we are in a stronger position to get this right and to operate from a place of trust and confidence, rather than fear and apathy.

How can you develop your skills at building trust with others?

I'm not going to give you a toolkit for building simple rapport with others – telling you to smile, listen and nod isn't the purpose of this chapter. All of this is incredibly important if you don't want to appear an automaton, but I'm imagining you've got that cracked as an HR professional. The tips that follow focus on how you can build trust through your communication skills, approach and mindset.

Building and scaling trust requires being skilled in the following:

1. *Organisational knowledge* – understanding the priorities and needs of your organisation. This is absolutely key. It isn't about showing a general interest in what your organisation does, makes or sells. This is about understanding the market context, and what that means for its people, and applying all this knowledge to consider what part you can play in supporting their success.

2. *Listening to understand, and not to respond* – building trust requires us to have the self-awareness that we are not, and do not need to be, in expert mode to deliver impact for

our clients and stakeholders. You will become stronger at building trust through listening to others and giving them the space to think about what is important to them and the organisation. Creating an environment where people are listened to gives you greater opportunity to respond to other people's agenda, rather than to be seen to be forming your own.

3. *Practise empathy and role-model this within your organisation* – empathy, the ability to understand other's needs, motivations and drivers through their eyes rather than your own, is a key leadership skill and a key skill of any HR professional. Having empathy for others supports you in understanding why people may not respond favourably to your ideas and proposals and supports you to tailor these to the needs of different groups. It also gives you a greater human touch when difficult business decisions need to be made. I've certainly learned some difficult lessons myself when my well-intended decisions and processes have landed badly with people. Which leads me onto another key skill.

4. *Learning from our mistakes* – we're all human, we all make mistakes. A key part of a person-centred culture is where we can readily accept these mistakes and learn from them. Learning from our mistakes and being open to feedback is an incredibly important part of building trust. This can be difficult in HR when situations become contentious and we are advised not to 'admit to mistakes' as we enter formal processes. Wherever possible, we need to nip these issues in the bud, deal with them informally and say sorry where the impact of our decisions has negatively impacted people. We are not apologising here for having negative intent, for we're in a new world where we're committed to operating with a strong people focus; but it's only human to apologise and

to seek to remedy where such actions have caused pain to others.

5. *Building genuine trust requires courage* – I've already talked about the importance of questioning and offering challenge as we seek to be 'trusted advisers' to the business. I've also noted the importance of demonstrating humility, both in recognising our mistakes but also in operating without a sense of arrogance. I read recently that 'humility and courage are two sides of the same coin', and I think this is very true. Building trust will require the courage to put forward unpopular ideas and to challenge the organisation should it sway from its commitment to a people-centred culture when the external market becomes tough. You are building trust that you will operate with integrity and purpose even when this is challenging for you, and this will require you to step away from any desire to 'be liked' and seek to be a 'likeable person acting with purpose'. There's a subtle but important difference there. In Kim Scott's book, *Radical Candour*, she describes this as 'the act of caring very deeply about people, but never stepping back from difficult discussions that push people to continually improve'.

The concept of self-trust and applying this to support our HR practice

Self-trust supports us to continually calibrate our actions with our sense of self, our values and our beliefs, to ensure that we are operating authentically. Self-trust supports us to act without self-doubt and with a sense of self-assurance that inspires confidence in others. It also supports us to build trust more quickly with others, as they will respond to our own sense of self-knowledge that is cultivated through continual self-reflection.

What does this mean in practice for you as an HR professional?

1. *Treat yourself as an individual and give yourself time to reflect* – trust in your own knowledge, values and decision-making, and give yourself time to reflect on these when faced with a decision. The lack of time to reflect or to consider your own position can lead us toward a lack of trust in ourselves. Ensure you have the time and space to honour your own commitments to yourself, for example to work in a particular way with others.

2. *Seek supportive feedback to inform your choices* – surround yourself by a diverse mix of people that you trust to provide you with 'radical candour', such as Kim Scott proposes in her book of the same name.[36] Trust in yourself and seek to continually learn from your behaviours and the context and emotions that trigger these. We need to trust ourselves to respond in a person-centred way regardless of challenge and other contextual factors, and we can only achieve this if we continuously reflect on what happens to our behaviour in different contexts. We are only human too, and continual supportive feedback helps us to develop our professional practice.

3. *Being mindful as HR professionals* – trust in yourself to seek evidence to support your activities, and also to judge when you have sought sufficient evidence from reliable sources to inform your decision-making. I mention this under the topic of being 'mindful' because, for me, beyond its roots in meditative practice, it is about being present in the here and

---

[36] Scott, K. (2018). *Radical Candour: How to Get What You Want by Saying What You Mean.* Pan Books: London.

now. There is great temptation to adopt new fads and things to create swift change, but we need to trust in our ability to find more appropriate, sustainable answers, and deflect the challenge whilst we gather the evidence to inform these.

4. *Operate with self-compassion and a lack of judgement* – fostering self-trust involves developing compassion for ourselves. It is very easy to be unkind to ourselves when busy or under strain, but if we're to instil compassion within our cultures, we need to start with ourselves. Don't get caught within the busyness trap, and create space and the will to offer yourself a little compassion too. A person-centred culture is inclusive and doesn't deride others for a difference of opinion or for failure. Offer this lack of judgement to yourself too. Use your mistakes and challenges as an opportunity to learn, reflect and move on.

Summary

We have explored a range of topics in this chapter, all focused on how you can support and develop your sense of self, and how you bring yourself to your HR practice. In exploring your values and beliefs, how you build trust as an individual, and how you trust in your own actions, I hope we will be supporting how you consider your 'self as an instrument'. We can't be person-centred if we're not operating from a place where our sense of 'self' and what we bring to our work is at the centre of all we do. The toolkit that follows supports you to delve into your strengths, values and aspirations in a little more depth. You might also want to draw on the support of a strength-based psychometric and/or 360-degree feedback to gain further reflections.

Toolkit H: Considering your personal brand – your values, beliefs, strengths and aspirations

1. *Reflecting on your values.*

   We all have core values. When these values and beliefs are compromised, we tend to feel out of kilter, whilst when we are living in alignment with our values, we are more likely to feel in control and decision-making can feel easier.

   Values can include topics such as family, learning, faith, generosity, education fairness, professionalism, accuracy, compassion and kindness. You can view all of these areas as important, and indeed can invest much time and energy in them, but I'd suggest you try to isolate just three to four core values that serve to guide you in how you operate.

   You might like to start with a blank sheet of paper and to consider what is important to you, what guides you and what you care most about.

2. *Reflecting on your strengths or what energises you.*

   Having greater clarity of your strengths, in terms of what energises you, rather than where you're competent, will support you in making stronger choices and decisions about your personal and work life. It may also give you greater clarity about how you can apply your strengths to support your people, and to build people-centred cultures.

   In exploring this area, you may want to ask others about how they perceive your strengths, where your talents lie, and the difference they see that this makes to those around you.

3. *Reflecting on who and what you want to impact, and why.*
   Slightly different than values is to consider the legacy you would like to leave behind. Imagine that you're at the end of your life and have a chance to give your current self some advice. What would you say? We rarely stop to think about which things in our lives really matter the most to us, and why. Your priorities will shift and change throughout your life, so it can be useful to revisit this activity on a regular basis.

   I would suggest you follow a similar approach to when you brainstormed your personal values for this activity. Free-write as many different 'things' you would like to make an impact to or for, and why this is important to you. Then whittle this down into a shortlist and consider which would make the most compelling legacy for you. This should be based on what is important to *you* – try not to get caught up in social expectations, and what you feel you should do. Defining where you want to do your best work, or your life's work, is incredibly important and shouldn't be the realm of people-pleasing.

   This mini toolkit has offered you a brief framework for considering your values and strengths, and where you would like to focus your energies.

Chapter 9

Treating people like people through our processes and ways of working

Introduction

Working in HR isn't always easy. We're often called upon to deal with complex and sensitive issues in an organisation. People often say it's lonely at the top, and many can probably also confirm that it's lonely in standalone HR functions somewhere near(ish) to the top. There is a real opportunity in building a person-centred, more human HR function that we can reposition ourselves to be part of the business, partnering to build the future rather than enforcing corporate bureaucracy. Historically, HR has been able to wield quite a lot of power via its hefty manuals and policies, steeped in sufficient levels of employment law to appear untouchable. I'd like to propose that it's time for us to step away from the fixation on process, policy and procedure that still prevails in many HR departments and to focus on how we create fulfilling relationships with our people, and the much wider pool of people who may want to join or re-join our community again in the future. We need to embrace technology to support how we connect with people, and of course to support how we attract future talent. However, for all this talk about automation of processes and 'doing more with less', we also know that the 'human touch' still makes for a personalised and fulfilling experience for people. So, there is a balance to be struck here.

We need strong processes and systems; they support efficiency, fairness and clarity. However, strong processes can also be designed and applied in a way that enables and empowers people as individuals. The reality is that this approach is still progressive and not enough progress has been made. The tide has been turning though. There are an ever-growing number of organisations who are letting go of the command-and-control culture of yesteryear and embedding processes that trust in the person or people using them.

In this chapter, we won't labour through all the different HR processes you might find in the average HR team. My overriding advice would be to review what the core purpose of your HR team is and the core purpose of your organisation, and to truly assess how far your approach to policy and process embody both of these. It's startling how many organisations with values such as 'being bold' and 'innovation' are supported by a set of archaic HR policies that seek, or at least it would seem that way, to control the freedom and creativity of their people. 'Staff' (a word I often think is best left for Shepherds), are told when to be at work, some even 'clock-on' and they're at risk of a disciplinary if they're 'late' for being that innovative, bold person we're all looking for. Or perhaps they're reminded to be customer-focused and cheery, whilst given a strict 15-minute break and 'told off' for minor misdemeanours. I can still vividly remember a poster I used to pass as I clocked onto my shift at the café of a major supermarket brand. 'You're going on stage. Don't forget to smile.' I would have dearly loved to smile, but the prospect of a seven-hour shift with a despondent management team, and an eight-minute break to look forward to (once I made it to the canteen) didn't make the corners of my mouth spring into action. We need to reflect on how we embed HR processes and policies with 'heart' into positive employee experiences.

When I consider how we need to make the workplace more 'human', I'm not thinking of the workplaces that already offer a plethora of perks and 'thank you' incentives. They may well need a process shake-up too, but my focus is instead on those workplaces where people are akin to worker bees and the work isn't likely to be intrinsically motivating. Had I found making traffic-light jellies intrinsically motivating, I would have been one fortunate lady in that supermarket café. I made hundreds of the bloody things, my eyes blinking with tiredness from being out dancing with friends until the early hours. The only motivating thing in making those jellies was then sitting on the floor of the café with a colleague to eat one after lunch, which I suspect should have resulted in an HR process but was a pretty inexpensive motivator. If you haven't read *Hired* by James Bloodworth, please do. In fact, close this book, and give it a read. James is a gifted writer, journalist and researcher, and his book is about his experience of working in junior positions within a range of UK workplaces, including large online retailers and care homes. His book will remind you exactly why creating workplaces that respect and value their employees is a great, big burning platform for all of us. A great starting point is ensuring our policies, processes and practices reflect the type of culture we aspire to be.

So, what can we do as an HR team to put the human back into our Human Resources practices?

1. *Get in the mindset that we are treating people like people because it is the right thing to do* – we can't hide behind policies or legislation – we need to lead through our values and the belief that, regardless of adhering to 'what is legal', we will treat people like people because fundamentally it is the right

thing to do. Yes, of course, there is a business case, and a million statistics suggesting your employee 'productivity' will go through the roof, but they're seldom based on much more than shaky ground. The only evidence you really need is that human beings deserve to be treated with that magic word 'humanity'. That should spur you on.

2. *If you have a manual, throw it out* – save for a few essential policies or guidelines, there really is no toolkit for being a human in an organisation, nor for managing a human in an organisation. Build the capability and self-awareness of your people to lead and manage others; to delegate with trust, and to empower others to achieve what they need to. Hire people for their values, potentially ahead of even their technical skills, and build their capability to understand what it means to contribute within your organisation.

3. *Fairness is the cornerstone of all we do* – stay true to this, no matter what, and don't over-rely on what 'fair' might look like from a legal standpoint. Do you know you have acted fairly and with all the compassion and respect possible in a given situation? If so, happy days. I have experienced some challenging times at work when my own sense of fairness has been questioned, and I fully respect the rights of the people involved to challenge and question my approach. In truth, I challenged and questioned my approach more than anyone so that I could stay true to my values and the organisational values, and so that I could sleep at night knowing I had sought to 'do the right thing'. Fairness looks different from one person to another, so the law of course comes in pretty handy here, but we are always striving to be ethical, fair and just, and should also be striving to be kind in our approach. We won't always get this right, most certainly we won't be perceived to get it right by all, but it should be something we test ourselves on continuously in our professional practice.

4. *Replacing 'no' with 'what if?'* – in HR, we need to work with greater curiosity to find a 'yes' or at least considering 'what if', rather than policing our organisations to say 'no'. In building a person-centred culture and developing policies and processes that are person-centred, I would propose that we challenge every 'no' with a 'what if?' 'What if the 9–5, 5 days a week world is, or should be, on its way out?' 'What if my team member just needs to be with their family in the evening, and encouraging them to do so will pay back tenfold?' You get the point.

5. *Make people feel valued* – 'People will forget what you did. They will forget what you said. But they will never forget how you made them feel.' These are the beautiful words of Maya Angelou, a writer that embodied compassion, courage and heart beyond comparison. As an HR team, we should individually and collectively seek to make others feel valued, to feel fairly treated and to feel safe at work. It is ok, indeed better than ok, for us to be promoting positive, human-centred processes. We know we can be business-like and commercially minded, but that is perhaps not the greatest value that we can offer to our organisations.

6. *Stop 'doing stuff'* – my goodness it's tempting to 'do stuff'. There is nothing more enticing than a long action plan of 'things' to make us feel like we're creating impact at work. Sometimes we are, but more often we're getting 'intervention-itis', and these little fads fizzle out as quickly as you can say 'quick win'. So, in HR, I would propose that we would benefit from looking at the processes and the activities we are putting in place, and to really think about the evidence-base for doing this, and more importantly if our organisation needs it and for what purpose. In HR, we can often be like magpies as we search out the latest shiny

solution out there. We're often coming from a place of great, positive intent, but the outcome can be that nothing sticks, and we waste organisational money trying to embed a solution that just isn't needed.

7. *Ask people what good looks like to them* – when redesigning HR processes, really think about what people want and need. But bear in mind that what people verbalise that they want, won't always be progressive, or perhaps in line with your vision. So, show them what's possible. Excite them with how different the workplace could look.

8. *Re-educate your team to get on board with the change* – it's often been said to me, 'Not all HR people like people.' It seems a funny place to end up if that is in fact true, but I can imagine the role can be wearisome and you can't blame a person for lessening their love for people if all they do is take flack all day. That said, we're not going to change the nature of the workplace and the role of HR within it if everyone doesn't get on board and become part of this. Our vision for person-centred HR isn't going to be successful if your team are nodding their heads but they're not seeking to change the processes in your HR function.

Starting as you mean to go on – recruiting people in a people-focused way

People-focused leaders see hiring new people as a fantastic opportunity to build the skills of their team, and to develop a dynamic that will create results. This might seem obvious, but recruiting new people often comes at a point when you least need it, and perhaps least expect it. Your team are bubbling along really quite well and then suddenly someone resigns, or perhaps your team are internally combusting and then you're left with a big, gaping retention hole. Either way, no one relishes having an incomplete team. However, what you'll see people-focused leaders doing differently is constantly being on the lookout for people who can bring value to their team and to the wider organisation, and they take an active and interested role in building their own talent pipeline. This person is an HR person's dream; someone who sees recruitment as a true strategic people priority and treats people like people, and not a statistic to be added onto the staff list.

Putting the human into recruitment doesn't end with just thinking it's important though. Having a compassionate and caring approach to recruitment is about forming genuine connections with potential new hires and welcoming them into an experience at work that feels authentic. The wealth of technology available to automate aspects of the recruitment process and to support an efficient hiring process is brilliant and increasing by the week, but the bigger opportunity for those of us who want to put the human back into HR is to increase human interaction in the process. Recruitment professionals and business leaders who are able to connect with people on a human level, rather than viewing them as mere 'candidates', nurture a far more positive experience through the hiring process. One of the best recruitment experts I have ever worked with held technical skills in spades, but his true talent I believe was a keen and genuine interest in his so-called candidates as people, and bigger than that, as potential team members. He cared about how they might experience the culture, and if it were the right fit for them and for us, and I listened to him really investing time in getting to know people as people. This might seem a luxury to have the time to achieve this. Not at all. For he invested time in this activity and got the right people on board, so time spent managing underperformance or issues with team dynamics were minimal in the organisation.

How can we learn from people like my former colleague to build recruitment processes with heart?

1. *Get to know people as people and talk to them honestly and openly, rather than in soundbites* – we can all reel off a list of organisational values and our mission and vision to potential candidates. Success here will rely on the very basics of relationship-building; find out what is interesting or useful to the other person (the hook), and tailor your approach to this.

2. *Bring people into communities rather than into a role* – allow the candidate to understand the team and the environment they will be joining and allow them to meet that community before joining. This isn't just about having an 'informal' part of the recruitment process where you spin the potential new recruit past a few team members – show them the culture, warts and all, and let them know how they can be part of the community there.

3. *Communicate regularly with candidates as if you care, and you should care* – employers who don't respond to candidates quickly (or at all) damage their employer brand and put people off applying for future roles. I once went through a long application process and a video interview, only to chase up repeatedly and be told after six weeks an internal candidate had been given the role. This was for a senior level position within a relatively tight sector – it's just not worth getting wrong, as everyone ultimately knows each other and leaves with a pretty negative view of how your organisation operates. Ultimately, everyone has better things to do on a weekend than writing a covering letter for your job, so respect those people as human beings, value their leisure time, and let them know if they aren't successful. Gripe over.

4. *Treat the interview as an interview for both parties* – give your candidates as much information as possible to help them prepare for interview, so that again they can decide if they want to work for you. Helping candidates to operate at their very best also shows you care and that you are out to support people to succeed. Another interview gripe – I can remember once doing a video interview when I had thought it was an informal exploratory discussion about an associate role. I thought we were having a call so I could find out more about what their business was focusing on and how I might support it. It wasn't. It was a formal interview and I wasn't properly prepared. Whilst this was my own fault, and pretty embarrassing, what I recall more than anything is how cross the interviewer was that I couldn't reel their business areas and values off the tip of my tongue. An awkward interview process is awkward for all, and something to avoid.

5. *Seek feedback from candidates* – ask your candidates how they experienced your process. I will ask for feedback wherever I can get it. Look to continuously delight your potential recruits, and to continually learn from situations where that has not been the case.

6. *Remember, the power is not all yours* – it's so interesting how a recruiter's approach changes depending on the market. It is absolutely imperative that we remember that recruitment is all about building relationships, and though someone may not be right for the role you're recruiting for now, they might be a future hire for you. The world is also a surprisingly small place, so do remember the importance of treating everyone equally, with dignity and care throughout your recruitment process.

Beyond human capital and headcount – language that fosters humanity

We often hear organisations state that employees are their 'greatest assets'. What a horrible phrase. Assets are things like buildings, computer equipment and furniture. Surely, we don't equate our fellow human beings with mere equipment. I appreciate employers usually mean the word 'asset' in a positive sense, intending to communicate how important and valuable the people are to their success. I would suggest that the biggest problem with the phrase 'asset' is that it drives a particular mindset – one where we tend to view our employees as a homogenous lump we can buy and sell, rather than as the incredibly complex, messy and wonderful sentient beings they are. So, let's simply call our employees 'people' and stop counting 'heads' and adding to 'staff lists'. We often design new HR processes as if we are indeed dealing with one big homogenous lump of people. If I've utterly lost you at this point, and you're wondering how you're going to shift any cultures through considering your use of language, please remember just how powerful language is. It's hugely powerful – the words we use shape our thoughts and feelings, as much as our thoughts and feelings shape the words that we use. Our worlds are socially constructed – two people can experience the same lunchtime in the office restaurant in such wildly different ways, dependent on their previous experiences, their personalities, moods and also how they express these experiences through their choice of language. My knowledge of evolutionary psychology and speech was left behind in an exam hall sometime in 2001, and perhaps best left there, but I just want to make the point that how we refer to people really matters.

What could language with 'humanity' look like in practice? Beyond talking about people as human beings and not 'headcount', I believe we would benefit from speaking more openly about concepts, values and behaviours such as 'compassion' and 'empathy' in the workplace. Society, at least in the United Kingdom, is taking some steps forward in debunking myths about mental well-being and encouraging people to talk more openly about their mental health. There would be some benefit to us all speaking more openly about the importance of treating each other with kindness and compassion. Both topics require us to step away from 'professionalism equates to a stiff upper lip', in the United Kingdom in particular, and to consider that there really is another way. If I think back to some of the line managers or colleagues I would have worked through the night for or would have shouted out about their talent and potential to anyone who would listen, it is those who have demonstrated kindness or who have sought to tailor a situation to support me. This isn't purely because I have bias toward kindness and compassion, which I am aware I do, but because we humans need connection despite some of our better attempts to pretend that we really don't.

Creating employee recognition mechanisms that are empowering and not patronising

In further exploring how we can bring greater humanity into our people processes, it's definitely worth reviewing our reward and recognition strategies in Human Resources. It is generally accepted that we should recognise our people for performing well against expectations. The need for recognition is systematic in our business culture and is driven by the use of competency-based assessment and the need to identify talent and therefore to determine who is a high achiever and who is average or below. The reality is that most recognition schemes or talent identification schemes do very little to motivate or engage employees. These schemes typically highlight a minority, who again typically would have succeeded despite such formal recognition and highlight a majority who won't receive the same kudos or rewards and are now expected to bask in the soft glow of the term 'average', or, even better, 'solid contributor'. Recognition is now seen as a necessity in most people strategies and yet the need for it not only creates a population of people who feel vulnerable and insecure, it also creates rebellion and a 'them and us' situation when reward schemes are set in place to highlight a minority.

All that said, I clearly support the notion of recognising the performance and potential of people within organisations. I believe in giving people honest feedback and using all of these things to empower people and to treat them as adults. However, I believe to put the 'human' back into our Human Resources approaches, we need to build processes and practices that avoid an over-reliance on recognition. We're surely aiming to support motivated people who will happily get on with being high-achievers, rather than people who feel demotivated if they don't get the highest pay award? We want to tap into their intrinsic motivations, and sustain high performance, rather than to build a reliance on external recognition and reward. There is not a single person I have ever met that does not worry about what others think of them; that does not believe that they are not as confident as others think they are. We fill the gap this imposter syndrome leaves with clothes, qualifications, holidays, brand names and impressive business connections. We hope that these things will make us happy or will prove to others that we're credible and worthy of note. It is time to empower people through our recognition schemes; using recognition and reward to celebrate the individual strengths and achievements of our people.

Summary

This is an enormous topic for a single chapter, and indeed many of the sub-topics within this chapter would be worthy of a book all of their own. We have explored how we can review and enhance our people processes, as a core enabler of shifting our cultures and creating workplaces where people are 'people not paperclips'. This has been a great opportunity to consider how language in our policies and processes has a strong bearing on our culture. I am an enormous advocate for progressive policies and processes that drive flexibility, inclusion and trust. It is going to feel like a giant leap for some organisations to move away from their HR manuals or lengthy HR policies to just trust that their people will do the right thing. The toolkit that follows is intended to support you in prioritising how you can review your HR processes to make a step change into a person-centred culture. This is the final toolkit before we move into action to create person-centred cultures.

Toolkit I: Putting the human back into our HR processes

This toolkit will support you in considering how person-centred your people processes are, and will offer a simple model to review and reshape these.

1. *Reviewing your policies*
   The first step in reviewing how person-centred your HR processes are, and how person-centred you want them to be, requires you to map these out. Mapping out processes can be as simple as listing the processes, considering the key steps in each process, and deciding what and who each step involves.

Clearly, this toolkit won't offer a model for a sophisticated process redesign. However, I hope to support you in preparing for more detailed process redesign through doing some initial groundwork on how person-centred your current processes are. Ask the following questions for each people process – for example, recruitment – to get started:

- How do we engage with people throughout the process?

- How do we want them to feel throughout the process, and how do we demonstrate this?

- How do we seek feedback from all parties involved in the process?

- How will we measure whether this process has achieved whatever we're looking for? (What does person-centred need to mean in relation to this process, and why?)

- How will we know if we've been successful?

2. *Testing your processes with people that care (and people who will challenge you)*

I realise you'll test your proposed processes with others as a point of good practice, but I would urge you to really seek out conflicting views or feedback that will test and challenge any assumptions you might be making. Remember, we're seeking person-centred processes, and therefore these need to be inclusive and tailored to the needs of a range of people with very different needs and motivations. If the old adage 'you can't please all the people all of the time' is true, we're going to give it our best shot here.

Ask for people's feedback, but also ask how they will be supporting and driving a people-centred culture through these processes. For example, an onboarding process is more than a mere HR process. It is the way in which the leaders and employees of an organisation collectively welcome in new people and support them, helping them to navigate the organisation and to contribute to its success. Why does it matter if people care and if they will challenge you? These people are not 'yes' people; they are going to test and challenge how it works, and they are likely to be the people we will be calling on for the next phase – implementation.

3. *Implement and embed your processes in the manner in which you want them to be received*

If you want everyone to be inspired and excited by the renewed people focus you are bringing through your approach to reward and recognition, my goodness, think of a more inspiring way to share this than an employee newsletter or an email to all staff. Get people together to share stories about the difference this will make, share why you're excited about the change, and only then let people know how to find more detail to wade through at their leisure.

The process is not 'finished' when its published. This is the mere starting point for putting that process or policy into action. Gone are the days when we could put a set of guidelines on the intranet or on an email and point to it whenever a question arose. 'You have an individual seeking a more flexible working pattern? Please refer to policy and process X and Z, and fill in form Y.' There will be some form of information collation involved in most of your processes, but in putting them into action, think about how you can upskill in addition to informing your line managers and wider workforce of the intent and principles of these processes. Once formed, they are no longer yours. They shouldn't be 'HR processes' at all. These are people processes that will drive the success of the organisation and will be embedded by your people.

Redesigning processes can be an incredible kick-start for cultural change. Get excited about it and help others to see why they should be excited too!

SECTION FOUR

OVER TO YOU

Chapter 10

A call to action for HR professionals

So, why focus on 'humanising' our workplaces? And, why now? I hope I have painted a compelling case for creating cultures that care, and that recognise the importance of treating people like people. More so, I hope I have painted a picture for how Human Resources should and can lead the way in this change. We're supposedly the 'people-people', so it seems bonkers that we're busy totting up our engagement scores whilst failing to make any sizeable steps toward systemic cultural change. The profession is packed full of incredibly talented and committed people – there is a global workforce out there that I strongly suspect is tired of being classed as 'human capital', and we can change this.

If it becomes more than a useful doorstop or welcome distraction on your morning commute, I hope this book will inspire you to reflect on your own HR practice and the role you and your team or peers can play in leading this change. These final chapters offer you a further toolkit to draw on when considering your own 'people not paperclips' plan.

In doing so, I hope you see a shift in how you and others experience the HR department and the ways of working within your organisation. I would ask you to share your stories, to share your lessons learned and successes. I hope in some small way these stories can serve as a ripple effect that can shift the tide of our global epidemic of disengagement at work. Life is precious, and short. Let's create workplaces where people find meaning and aren't clock-watching their way to the weekend.

I would like to share one final toolkit with you. This toolkit focuses on building your own OD plan for your organisation, an OD plan that focuses on how you can create a person-centred culture in your workplace and spur on our work to ensure people are treated like 'people not paperclips'. This toolkit is a blank framework for you to populate with your team and your stakeholders and focuses on what change you can instigate and facilitate at the individual level, team level and organisational level. There is a real tendency in HR to focus mainly on the first two levels through individual learning and team development workshops. I hope this book has illustrated how we need to align all our activities across all levels of the organisation to achieve meaningful change, and that working at the organisational or system level is an exciting place to be.

Your 'people not paperclips' plan

Before populating Diagram 1, which contains a framework for a high-level OD plan, consider the following in relation to *creating a person-centred culture* in your workplace:

Why change?

- What are the drivers for change?

- Who is driving the change, and why? (*Whilst it is brilliant if you are a catalyst for this all-important change, you can't drive it alone. Consider who else needs to drive the change, and how you will influence them to lead it with passion and energy.*)

- What difference will the change make, and how do you know this? (*This is your arsenal for influencing the people identified above.*)

- If you don't shift to a person-centred culture, so what? (*You know the answer to this. Organisations are moving at a pace, and people are ever discerning in selecting their future employers. Why would people choose to be treated like automatons over individuals with human needs? It would defy every motivation theory we've explored.*)

What is your organisational context – the enablers, barriers and interdependencies?

- What will support you to build a person-centred culture? (*Strong senior level buy-in? Employees demanding it? A strong business and person case for change?*)

- What may act as a barrier to achieving a person-centred culture? (*Lack of senior level buy-in? Understanding what it means in practice? Change fatigue, and people's readiness to embrace new ways of working?*)

- What else is happening within your organisation that you will need to consider when driving a person-centred culture? (*Embedding of values and behaviours? Developing your customer value proposition, and an opportunity to readdress how you talk about your culture? A review of ways of working? Implementing agile working? Whatever it is, there will doubtless be great opportunities to leverage your success through integration of key priorities.*)

How do you aim for the process to look and feel? What are the opportunities to drive change through the process itself?

- OD interventions do not need to be 'yet another project'. You can achieve change through the process itself. If you aim to introduce a stronger people focus in your organisation with a greater emphasis on compassionate leadership, you could start with a process like this:

○ Develop compassionate leadership in your executive team, and ask them to role-model these values and behaviours in how they talk to their teams about the importance of a person-centred culture.

○ Create open dialogue and trust within teams by building what 'person-centred' looks like through an open conversation with your people. More time-consuming perhaps, but again this is a powerful way of building trust through your process.

○ Develop open feedback through embedding feedback skills alongside development/skills in curiosity, strategic thinking and coaching skills (for questioning and challenge skills). The skills you build to support the process will build your organisational capability to sustain the change.

○ Ensure this is not viewed as an HR intervention. Being person-centred is seeing the organisation as being interconnected as a living system.

How will you engage your stakeholders to support the OD plan?

• Who do you need to gain early buy-in from, and who are your key influencers? (After identifying them, you will of course review who is best placed to support the 'entry and contracting phase'. Who will connect you to these people if you do not already hold strong credibility with them?)

- When and how will you engage key stakeholders? (In considering this, remember that all employees are stakeholders, and you do need a clear plan for how you will engage key groups or people with particular viewpoints within the employee group. So much time is spent on senior level engagement, which sometimes means 'employees' are just told about what is happening.)

- What communication channels are available to you to support engagement? If the formal channels are weak, or weak in places, how can you make stronger use of informal channels? (Remember that the lines, 'I put it on the intranet' and 'We sent an email' might as well read, 'Most people don't have a clue'.)

- Who else can you collaborate with to support the plan? (Be creative here and think of all the hidden voices or unlikely voices you could use to bring diversity of thought to your work.)

How will you know your OD plan has been successful?

- This question takes us back to how you will evaluate the success of your approach/process and how you will evaluate the outcome. Who will you seek feedback from? Where will you be drawing evaluation data from, and why? How valid and reliable is this data, and how do you know this?

- Is there a known 'exit' point for the OD plan, or a key review date?

These questions are intended to support you in crafting an OD plan that will build a 'people not paperclips' culture. It can be applied to any OD approaches, and indeed to any change you wish to create or support. Diagram 1.0 outlines a framework to capture your 'people not paperclips' plan. If you're adept in programme management, you may have already created a framework that will put mine to shame. Create something that is meaningful to you – this is a place to outline where you will prioritise dialogue and activity, and not a test of your MS Project skills!

Diagram 1.0: A basic framework to support 'people not paperclips' planning

Your 'people not paperclips' plan					
What is your vision? Articulate it here in one to two sentences.					
	How will you explore the change required at this level?	**What change will you create at this level? (Synthesis of exploration phase.)**	**How will you evaluate your success?**	**What key activities will take place?**	**When will activities be implemented?**
Individual level (change within employees, leaders, you as an HR professional)	*Speaking with employees, reviewing evidence and research*	*What will you see, hear, feel?*	*Be specific and ensure this is measurable, or at least can be shared*	*These need to be realistic and evidence-based, e.g. leadership development interventions*	*'What gets measured, gets done' etc....*
Team level (change within individual teams, between key teams)	*Consider how teams currently operate*				
Organisational level	*Organisation redesign, reviewing policies, processes and practices*				

Chapter 11

Summary

I am aware that this book merely scratches the surface of all that behavioural science and OD have to offer the topic of humanising our workplaces. If you've made it this far, you've managed to get over the fact it's not an academic text, but it also isn't quite a business book. It's a collection of key topics, references and suggestions for creating person-centred cultures, or work environments where people are treated like 'people not paperclips'. I've worked on the basis of 'done, not perfect' with this book. And I hope that you will work on the basis of 'done, not perfect' as you continue to develop your awareness and knowledge of behavioural science and OD; and as you continue to apply your thinking to create person-centred cultures at work. 'Done, not perfect' – what a liberating, person-centred approach.

When I found occupational psychology as a seventeen-year-old A-level student, I knew I'd found what I wanted to do and a topic I would never tire of. I felt the same way when I found Organisation Development, another profession built on humanistic principles and where practitioners share a genuine and deep curiosity to understand the human mind and human experience. I've applied my learning in both professions within Human Resources functions and within strategy departments aligned to it. It's been interesting, and at times bewildering, to see how some people can work in functions called 'People' whilst seemingly demonstrating scant interest in what motivates and engages those 'people'. Thankfully, this has shifted a great deal over the last 10 to 15 years, but there is still a long way to go. I love Human Resources. I love the ambition and the diversity that exists in this profession; the third profession I have felt lucky to call my own.

Do stay in touch and keep me informed as you achieve successes, or perhaps experience struggles, as you make sense of the change you can create in shifting your workplace to be truly 'person-centred'. You can find me at www.heartsparks.co.uk or at kath@heartsparks.co.uk. I still work in-house within Human Resources and OD because I love being part of a culture and contributing to causes that I care about as an internal consultant. Through my company, HeartSparks, I also continue to offer Organisation Development consultancy and coaching support across sectors, which includes building OD capability within HR teams.

Thanks for picking up this book and for staying the journey with me. Just the fact you picked it up gives me great hope that there are many like-minded people who want to use their expertise and their passion to make a difference. Please join me in giving a voice to every disengaged, overtired, underappreciated employee out there. To use the words of Gandhi again, let's 'be the change we want to see in the world'.

Further reading/Helpful websites

This further reading list is not exhaustive by any means. It is a list of interesting and useful books that I hope will continue to inspire you as you embark on your 'people not paperclips' plan.

Chahel, K. (2016). *Compassionism: Helping Business Leaders Create Engaged Teams and Happy People.* Panoma Press: St Albans.

- This book is a brilliant introduction to how to communicate with greater compassion at work. It's straightforward and accessible, and I wish I had been the one to coin the term 'compassionism'. I couldn't love it more.

Cheung-Judge, M-Y. and Holbeche, L. (2011). *Organisation Development: A Practitioner's Guide for OD and HR.* Kogan Page: London.

- Two absolute gurus in OD sharing their expertise in a practical guide. I'm embarrassed to say I have a 'Top 5 of Textbooks' chart, but I'm not embarrassed to say this is on there.

Worline, M. (2017). *Awakening Compassion at Work: The Quiet Power that Elevates People and Organisations.* McGraw-Hill Education: Delhi.

- This book outlines four steps for building compassion into the structures and practices of an organisation, which is a strong step toward driving cultural change. I'd suggest it's written for a knowledgeable audience, so if you're a senior HR professional, it might be right up your street. It's less chatty in style than this book, which might also be a relief to you…!

Websites you might find interesting in exploring these topics further:

- The Institute of OD: https://instituteod.com/ (Home of the OD Profession, relatively newly formed).

- Roffey Park: www.roffeypark.com (Roffey Parks runs some brilliant workshops and brilliant research in the fields of HR and OD).

- The Compassion Lab: www.thecompassionlab.com/about-us/ (a group of organisations researching and reporting on compassion at work, and on building organisations that treat people like individuals. You will find some brilliant resources here).

Printed in the USA
CPSIA information can be obtained
at www.ICGtesting.com
JSHW012031140824
68134JS00033B/2985